TAPPAN
ON
SURVIVAL

MEL TAPPAN

Foreword by
Bruce D. Clayton, Ph.D.

Paladin Press • Boulder, Colorado

Tappan on Survival
by Mel Tappan

Copyright © 1981 by Nancy M. Tappan

ISBN 13: 978-1-58160-509-9
Printed in the United States of America

Published by Paladin Press, a division of
Paladin Enterprises, Inc.
Gunbarrel Tech Center
7077 Winchester Circle
Boulder, Colorado 80301 USA
+1.303.443.7250

Direct inquiries and/or orders to the above address.

All photographs by Marv Wolf, unless otherwise credited.
Designed by Irene Friedman.

Visit our Web site at www.paladin-press.com

Foreword to Reprint Edition

by Bruce D. Clayton, Ph.D.

When I was 20, I became interested in survival skills for the most prosaic of reasons: I was hungry.

It was 1970, and I had a job at a summer-stock theater in Monterey, California, that included bed, board, and the munificent sum of $7 per week. The "board" consisted of one free meal a day at the local Armenian restaurant, where zucchini was regarded as *the* essential food group. After a few weeks, I just couldn't face another plate of steamed squash and began to forage for edible plants along the railroad tracks, in vacant lots, and along the seashore. It wasn't very productive, but it was fun.

With the help of a few like-minded friends (mainly from the same theater), I began to study survival skills. Within a couple of years I became a graduate student in biology, involving frequent, solitary trips into the remote wilderness of Montana and Idaho. When the forest is your office, you report for work rain or shine, winter and summer, and you usually go alone. A dead battery, a smashed oil pan, a sprained ankle, a snakebite: these simple things can kill you when you are 60 miles from the nearest phone. Wilderness survival skills became a real part of my life. Once again, preparedness turned out to be fun.

During graduate school, a professor asked me to prepare a seminar on the biological impact of a full-scale nuclear war. I plunged into the research, and my life took an unexpected turn. The danger of nuclear war was quite real in the 1970s. The leaders of the Soviet Union were elderly ideologues committed to the triumph of communism through the destruction of the United States. They had absolutely *huge* arsenals of nuclear, biological, and chemical weapons at their disposal, all aimed at us. A war unleashing such weapons would change civilization, perhaps even suspend it.

At the biological level, however, the world would not end. With some special knowledge and equipment, a well-prepared person could survive side-by-side with the hardiest animals, plants, and insects. Most of the challenge involved scaling up wilderness survival strategies into long-term solutions. Not food for a week, but food for a year. Not collecting berries, but planting orchards. Not a canteen of water, but a 5,000-gallon tank. Not a tent and a parka, but a snug house and cords of firewood. The sheer scale of the challenge made it irresistible.

My theater friends had scattered to several states by then, so our research was conducted in letters. We generated hundreds of pages of correspondence. One spring we all went on vacation together to discuss the kind of preparations we might be able to make. One of our members reached into his backpack and pulled out a book. "Have you guys seen *Survival Guns*?" he asked. That was my introduction to Mel Tappan.

Until that moment, we had not realized that preparing for long-term survival was a widespread phenomenon. Tappan's book showed us the world of "retreaters," soon to be renamed "survivalists." We had been survivalists for years and hadn't known it.

We devoured that book.

* * *

Survival Guns was a tour de force, a genuine masterpiece. It stands as a monument to Mel Tappan's unique personality. The book—as well as *Tappan on Survival*, the one you now hold in your hands—reveals a wonderful confluence of skillful writing, aggressive curiosity, fanaticism, wealth, and wisdom. Let's take those one at a time . . .

- Mel's impact was due in part to his powerful and engaging writing. It is just plain *fun* to read his books, his newsletters, and his *Guns & Ammo* columns, especially when he replied to critical letters. He loved the ones that started, "I wagered 50¢ with my husband that you would not print my letter . . ."

- Mel's curiosity extended into every aspect of preparedness. He wasn't content with generalities or solutions that were "good enough." He wanted to get his hands dirty and try it himself. His recommendations were based on experience, not theory. (Besides a lengthy chapter on firearms, *Tappan on Survival* contains information on everything from food storage and two-way radios to snakebite kits and watches.)

- He was fanatical about the danger of irresponsible banking practices. In the mid-1970s, Mel predicted that the banks would soon fail and civilization would collapse. Was he too paranoid? His concerns were borne out a decade later during the savings and loan crisis, although somehow civilization muddled through (after a huge bailout by the U.S. government).

- Most survivalists suffer from a chronic lack of funds, but Mel didn't seem to have that problem. If a friend recommended a new pistol to him, Mel would buy one and try it out. In fact, he would sometimes buy five of the same gun from different outlets to see if the gun maker's quality control was up to expectations. This kind of aggressive acquisition gave him a unique perspective that the rest of us couldn't hope to duplicate.

- And wisdom? Mel's wisdom is his greatest legacy to his readers: he had a special ability *to ask the right question*. Twenty years later, a few of the answers may have changed, but that's not a problem. Anybody can find an answer given enough time to do the research. The trick is to ask the right question in the first place so you aren't just spinning your wheels in wasted effort.

One incident sums up Mel Tappan for me. He mentions it about halfway through *Tappan on Survival*. Mel was often consulted about choosing the "best" weapons for defense. People's lives were at stake, so Mel didn't compromise on his research. He amassed an encyclopedic knowledge of defensive firearms.

Out here in California, we have a government that is obsessed with banning "assault rifles." Unfortunately, these bureaucrats have no idea what an "assault rifle" actually is. They have banned a long list of firearms that have black plastic stocks, folding stocks, bayonet lugs, flash suppressors, detachable magazines, or pistol grips . . . in other words, Hollywood's idea of a scary-looking gun. Tappan regarded these superficial appurtenances as being beside the point. A defensive weapon must have one quality before all others, he said: it must be *reliable*. A defensive weapon must keep firing as long as you still have enough blood pressure to move the trigger. It has to shoot and shoot and shoot, because if it fails, so will you.

Mel's research led him to a high opinion of the Heckler & Koch Model 91 rifle. Firing the 7.62 NATO round, the HK91 had everything survivalists needed in a battle rifle, he said. It had range, penetration, accuracy, and, above all, reliability. But just *how* reliable was it? Mel decided to find out.

At that time, an HK91 assault rifle cost more than $1,000. (The rifle goes for $2,000 to $3,000 today.) The price tag was beyond my reach, but Mel could afford it. In fact, he bought *three* of these rifles so he could report on their variability out of the box. He took his new rifles out to the firing range and determined that two would shoot sub-minute-of-angle groups (less than 1 inch wide at 100 yards) without any tuning, and one could make 3/8-inch groups at 100 yards. He was very pleased with this degree of accuracy, but he knew that accuracy often detracts from reliability. Were the HKs as reliable as they were accurate?

Mel borrowed a pile of 20-round magazines from his many friends and assembled a team of assistants to load them. Then—and this is the amazing part—he did his best to *destroy* one of these expensive rifles by firing 900 rounds through it as fast as he could bring the sights back on target after each shot. At 50 shots per minute, that's 18 minutes of continuous fire. His assistants scurried to keep full magazines at his elbow.

At the end of the experiment, Mel reported, the barrel of the gun was "hot enough to sear flesh" but the rifle had not misfired. He then fired a five-shot group at a target 230 yards downrange and punched a 4-inch group. Point of aim and accuracy were still satisfactory, even after the brutal abuse.

But he wasn't done! As a final test, Mel loaded a magazine with alternating layers of cartridges and *toothpaste* (to simulate mud) and fired it off. The HK loaded, fired, and ejected every cartridge flawlessly. Only then would Tappan endorse the weapon to his readers.

* * *

Mel was one of very few people to read the draft manuscript of *Life After Doomsday*, my manual on nuclear war survival. That was in 1978. I asked him to review it because of his formidable expertise, and he graciously agreed. He was very encouraging, and his remarks showed that he had studied the manuscript with typical Tappan thoroughness. He shared my concern about the Soviets, but he felt that economic collapse was the more pressing threat. For the most part he let the manuscript stand unchanged, while I hastily incorporated the suggestions he did make. A few months later, I became a guest columnist for his *Personal Survival Letter*, the premier survival newsletter of that age.

This was during the Carter administration, and the headlines of late 1979 and 1980 had to do with the Ayatollah Khomeini and the revolution in Iran, during which the U.S. Embassy was overrun and more than 52 Americans were taken hostage for 444 days. Under Carter's leadership, the United States proved completely ineffective at meeting this crisis. The Soviet Union invaded Afghanistan in December 1979, which seemed like a first step toward seizing the oil of the Persian Gulf. At the same time, the deregulation of the savings and loans industry began, which was the start of a long slide in which a thousand S&Ls went bankrupt just a few years later. The nightly news ran frequent, alarming stories about double-digit inflation. In early 1980, U.S. forces mounted a raid into Iran to rescue the hostages. It was a disaster—our guys encountered a dust storm in the desert and had to turn back. We lost aircraft and soldiers in the confusion. America was humiliated.

As a result, 1980 was a "boom" year for the survival movement. Survival books sold by the thousands. Dozens of survival newsletters and hundreds of supply companies emerged. I've never seen royalty checks like the ones I got that year for *Life After Doomsday*. People built fallout shelters and organized survival groups. Television crews from all corners of the world showed up at my house for interviews. It was a very exciting time.

And then something happened that took all the light out of it. Mel Tappan passed away, quite suddenly, on November 2, 1980. His death left a void that his friends couldn't ignore and couldn't fill. He left a desk piled high with unanswered letters.

Two days after Mel's death, on November 4, 1980, Ronald Reagan defeated Jimmy Carter and became president-elect of the United States. Reagan's hard-line rhetoric made America seem strong again. On January 20, 1981, Reagan was sworn in and delivered his inaugural address. The hostages in Iran were released only 20 minutes later.

Mel's disappointed readers continued to clamor for every remaining scrap of his knowledge, and in 1981 Nancy Tappan brought out *Tappan on Survival*, a collection of Mel's monthly columns from *Guns & Ammo* and *Soldier Of Fortune* magazines. The survival community warmly welcomed the book.

The next few years saw the collapse of the savings and loan bubble, but somehow we survived that and learned a few hard lessons. After almost 10 years of occupation, Soviet troops took a terrible beating in Afghanistan and had to withdraw in 1988–1989. Saddam

Hussein got frisky and invaded Kuwait, but the Desert Storm coalition had no trouble throwing him out. In 1991 the Soviet Union collapsed, and even nuclear war faded as a realistic threat to America.

Beginning in the early 1990s and continuing throughout the decade, a new danger lurked in the shadows, but we were not paying attention. Islamic radicals turned their anger and hatred toward the United States and trained terrorists from around the world to conduct attacks on U.S. citizens and installations. They set off a bomb under the World Trade Center in New York in 1993 (6 killed, 1,000 injured). They destroyed the Khobar Towers apartment complex (housing U.S. military personnel) in Saudi Arabia in 1996 (20 killed, 372 injured). They bombed the U.S. embassies in Kenya and Tanzania in 1998 (200 killed, 1,000 injured). They tried to sneak a bomb into Los Angeles for Christmas. Somehow, the American public just didn't take these collective news stories seriously. Terrorists? What terrorists?

Of course, we *were* distracted, this time by a crisis of our own making: the Y2K date-rollover computer glitch. Experts warned us that older software might suddenly fail when the date changed from 1999 to 2000. The faulty software was declared to be present in almost every electronic device, from toasters to automobile ignitions to nuclear power plant control panels. Dire Y2K predictions spurred a renewed interest in emergency preparedness. People started stocking up on food and equipment again. Everyone held their breath as the last seconds of 1999 ticked away. We were all watching the news at midnight when . . .

. . . nothing happened. The clocks kept right on ticking. The lights stayed on. Traffic kept moving. The sun came up on schedule. We spent the next day watching New Year's Day parades and football games, just like always.

When the Y2K bug fizzled, the unprepared masses had a good laugh at the expense of the people who had "wasted" their money preparing for it. I had taken the opportunity to install a powerful propane generator to keep my home and business running in case the power grid went down. I didn't need the generator for Y2K, but that doesn't mean it was wasted. We have blackouts several times a year here. When we do, I take a certain pleasure in turning on all the floodlights while the rest of the neighborhood is fumbling around in the dark.

In the summer of 2000, Americans watched in horror as people ate slugs for a million-dollar prize on the *Survivor* show. Ironically, this game show was billed as "reality TV." We barely noticed the near-sinking of the USS *Cole* that fall, the victim of a suicidal *jihadi* in a speedboat.

Then, in 2001, al-Qaida radicals hijacked some airplanes and immolated themselves along with a big chunk of Wall Street and the Pentagon. As the Twin Towers collapsed, "reality TV" suddenly collided with reality. Confronting the Islamic threat at last, the American government sent troops to Afghanistan in pursuit of Osama Bin Laden, whom they said we would quickly bring to justice. At the time of this writing, he has continued to elude capture.

In March 2003, U.S. and Coalition forces went into Iraq, quickly toppling Saddam Hussein's government. However, three years later they are still fighting an insurgency, and no Iraqi government has yet been formed.

Now we worry about . . . what? Our new Department of Homeland Security (DHS) is running amok over our basic freedoms while neglecting disaster preparedness. The Federal Emergency Management Agency (FEMA), a part of DHS, completely botched the response to Hurricane Katrina. FEMA's advice on terrorism was no better: officials told us to stock up on duct tape and rolls of plastic sheeting. In the event of a biological, chemical, or radiological attack, we won't be safe, but at least we'll be able to make our own body bags. People are not feeling reassured.

If that were not enough, our old enemies in Iran are on the move again. The mullahs are working hard to build their own nuclear weapons, and their pathological leaders have once again announced that America must perish. These Iranian zealots are a much greater threat than al-Qaida or the Palestinian teenagers who blow up buses for Allah. For one thing, Iran already possesses ballistic missiles that can reach as far as Paris. If the Iranians decide to target something, it will be bigger than a bus. It could be a lot bigger.

That's why people are starting to read those dusty old survival books again.

There are those who will say that *Tappan on Survival* is dated, that it doesn't contain the latest, up-to-the-minute dope on survival equipment for the 21st century. Mel wrote these columns 25 years ago, so that accusation is partly true. It also misses the point.

Reading these articles again, I see more important things than just the latest fashions in firearms. I see long-term survival presented by a master in terms of priorities and criteria, with an unrelenting emphasis on pragmatism. As you read Mel's columns, you can feel him inside your mind, taking hold of your most cherished ideas and shoving them around like furniture in an untidy room. Suddenly everything fits, and you can see how to proceed on your own. More than any other writer, Mel Tappan taught us how to *think* about survival. That's what this book can do for you.

If you are new to Mel's work, I envy you. In a world of savage enemies, you are about to make a formidable new friend.

Bruce Clayton
February 2006

Bruce Clayton is the author of *Life After Doomsday* (1980), *Thinking About Survival* (1984), *Fallout Survival* (1984), and *Life After Terrorism* (2002), all from Paladin Press. His latest book is *Shotokan's Secret* (2004) from Black Belt Books.

Table of Contents

ACKNOWLEDGEMENTS

I am grateful to Petersen Publishing Company and to Omega Group Limited for permission to reprint the material in this book. The first chapter appeared in the December, 1980, and January, 1981, issues of *Soldier of Fortune* and the remaining chapters in *Guns & Ammo* from February, 1977, to June, 1980. The guns used in the photo on page 78 were courtesy of T.H. Klein & Co., El Toro, California. I also wish to thank Dr. John Robbins of Congressman Ron Paul's office and Grant Manning of Radio West for their help in updating information in chapters one and six respectively.

Without the perceptive, intelligent help of Candice Kindred this manuscript would never have reached the printer. And, of course, without Mel's material there would have been no manuscript.

FOREWORD

by Jerry Pournelle

There aren't many people who change your life. Mel Tappan was one who did. As I sit here in my Hollywood office I can reach out and put my hand on a dozen objects I wouldn't have if Mel hadn't written his books and columns.

Life-Tool from Allison Forge Corporation. A handy-dandy patent axe sharpener that has saved hours of work. The magazine extension on my Remington 870. Sight adjustment tools for the H&K. Radios, and — —

Amazing. All that gadgetry. Still, gadgets don't change your life; yet Mel Tappan changed mine. He got me to think seriously about survival.

Not that I hadn't thought about it before. My family has always known what to do and where to go in case of nuclear war. I've always owned my share of equipment, I'm the hikemaster for our local Boy Scout troop, and my normal car is a four-wheel drive truck. I've even got a few friends who look to me for instructions in case things get sour.

But for all that I was playing at survival. It took Mel to make me really think about the problem.

Not that I agreed with all of his attitudes and prejudices. In our rather frenzied telephone exchanges it was clear we'd never really agree. He saw civilization as hopelessly doomed. Collapse was inevitable, and the only prudent thing to do was to be prepared for it.

I didn't agree then, and I don't now. I think civilization can be saved. Can be. But I won't guarantee it. Be Prepared is a pretty good motto for anybody, scouts or anyone else.

And of course there are times when I think Mel was right. If you have any doubts about the possibility of civilization's collapse after reading this book, try Roberto Vacca's *The Coming Dark Age*; or just read the headlines and think of how many buttons there are, and what fingers rest on them . . .

No. Even when you disagree with Tappan, you must take him seriously; which, I suspect, is as much as he ever wanted.

* * *

It began with a telephone call from Theodore Sturgeon. He wanted to recommend a book he'd just finished. It was called *Survival Guns*, and he hadn't been able to put it down. I thought this rather odd, because although Ted Sturgeon is and can be a ruggedly self-sufficient chap, he isn't what you'd call your typical firearms freak.

"Practical advice and cold logic," Ted said. "You read it."

The only difficulty was that I had no opportunity to read it; this was well before the survivalist boom, and Mel's book wasn't often displayed for sale. I was working on *Lucifer's Hammer* just then, and had little time for outside reading anyway. I promptly forgot Ted's recommendation until *Hammer* was in the hands of the publishers. Not long after that I happened to see *Survival Guns* somewhere, probably in a gun store, and I bought it — —

And read it in one marathon sitting, wishing I'd had it while doing *Hammer*. Not that I'm ashamed of the survival scenes in *Hammer*. Not at all. They're drawn from personal experiences, often written in the places they happened; and I have good reason to believe it was reasonably well done, as you'll see in a moment.

Do understand. I grew up in Tennessee, in a time when you really could go off into the wilderness with a blanket roll and an axe and a skillet, some johnny-cake mix, a rifle, and a handful of cartridges, and live quite well for a couple of weeks. Not that I did that often—but I have done it. And I've been reading Horace Kephart's *Camping and Woodcraft* (a book first written in 1915; my present well-worn copy is the 25th printing, MacMillan, 1968) since I was nine. I don't hunt much any more, but I used to, and I still take the scouts into the High Sierra every summer.

vi

I've been a soldier, and I've put in some time in fairly strange places. I thought I knew a lot about guns, and how to take care of myself.

But I soon learned that Mel Tappan knew a lot more. He'd done a lot of thinking and a lot of research. He could also write; write clearly, interestingly, compellingly. When I agreed with him I found myself nodding enthusiastically. Other times I was ready to shout defiance. No, dammit, it's not that way — —

But even disagreeing was pleasurable, because it made me think about the subject. It's surprising how much of what you think you *know* turns out to be prejudice. Sometimes very old prejudice.

Example. When I was first issued a combat weapon, many and many a year ago, the armory sergeant handed me a Colt .45. I lifted it experimentally and listened to the barrel rattle around against its bushing. "Nothing better?"

He shrugged. "No, sir. Got some worse ones. Maybe this will help." He took out a length of parachute cord. "Tie that around the trigger guard and give 'er that," he said, indicating that I should swing the piece around and around my head. "You'll probably do about as well — —"

An attitude I shared, and I felt a bit smug about the .357 revolver I had in my ki . . .

But there was Mel Tappan telling me that the .45 Colt auto was the finest defensive pistol ever made, and giving me some pretty good reasons; and also telling what to have the gunsmiths do to the piece.

Could he be right? I was ready to concede that he knew guns. After all, he'd praised the Remington 870, and I had one because I too thought it about the best shotgun ever made. He said nice things about the M1 Garand. He liked the FN without worshipping it, and I'd had a bit of experience with those. He liked the Chief's Special, which had been my choice for a concealable piece back when I needed something inconspicuous. And he knew about the Winchester Model 70, and that the older ones (like my 1958 30-06) were better made than the newer editions . . .

Which was interesting: in those cases where I could claim reasonable knowledge, I found Tappan in agreement. Which meant that he ought to be listened to in the cases I didn't know much about. Such as the .45 auto.

So, what the hell, I thought, let's try it. After all, it has been twenty-five years since they handed me that lump of iron in Pusan. So off to the gunshop, with a list of the modifications recommended by Tappan, and — —

And, all right, so he was right, of course, and now I own two Mark IV's, and I gave one to my daughter for her birthday.

There was a lot to think about in *Survival Guns*.

Before I was through digesting its lessons, I had bought five more firearms, two scopes, a locker full of ammunition, and a peach crate full of spare parts. But Mel wasn't through with me yet.

* * *

I write books for a living. Fortunately they sell pretty well, giving me the opportunity to get out and do research. Most times I live what I write about. But nobody can know everything, and I do sometimes have to work from printed materials, particularly magazines and periodicals.

I have a strange system. I subscribe to a *lot* of magazines. The justification is that I hate to read in libraries, and if I ever get just one really good idea from one issue, that will pay for the subscription for a long time.

The magazines come in, and when I can I glance at them, and otherwise my long-suffering associate files them, keeping current issues around the office and archiving the back issues in the increasingly full dead storage area of the attic.

The back cover of *Survival Guns* mentioned that Mel Tappan was a columnist for *Guns & Ammo* magazine, but I hadn't noticed that. I can't think why. So a year went past...

I was writing *Janissaries*, a novel which featured some

modern-day mercenary soldiers. They were to be equipped with fairly modern weapons, and nobody can keep up with everything; I figured I'd better do some reading. So up to the dusty archives I skipped to drag down all my back issues of *G&A* and also *American Rifleman*; and on opening *G&A* I found Mel's column.

That shot the whole day as I went back and read every column he'd done. They were full of good stuff, suggestions for equipment, advice, thought pieces, recommended books; all kinds of stuff. And certainly he hadn't lost his ability to argue: even when I didn't agree I found myself thinking hard about what he'd said.

So I sat down and wrote him a fan letter.

A week later the phone rang. It was Mel Tappan, who had read *Lucifer's Hammer* and *The Mercenary* and a couple of my other books, and had been thinking of writing *me* a fan letter — —

Thus began a pleasurable friendship. It was all too brief.

* * *

Time passed. Mel sent me copies of his *Personal Survival Letter*, whose motto was "Starts where other newsletters leave off" and lived up to it. (It's being continued by Nancy and Mel's associates, and still does.) And once in a while we'd talk on the phone again, sometimes to argue, sometimes to agree. I took him to task for his attitude about axes; when I was a kid, an axe or hatchet were practically sacred, since it took many hours to sharpen one properly (the method is given in Kephart) and only seconds to ruin one. To Mel they were just tools, to be bought in quantity and ruined if need be. But of course he'd found this tool that could actually sharpen a new store-bought axe (they all have heavy cheeks and jowels that make them useless as bought) . . .

Darned tool works, too. I still haven't quite got over my attitude. I still reverently put my axe away after I use it. But Mel did have a point . . .

And we talked about other things. Backpacking rigs (he

wasn't much for Backwoods Batmen, and I don't think he ever did read Kephart. Pity.) Cars, radios, gadgets, skills. Where to go, comes That Day, and what you can do to stay alive; and whether we'll have That Day, and if so, what will bring it about, and whether we can stop it from coming at all. (I said we could. Mel thought not.)

In other words, we talked about all the things you'll find in this book, which Nancy Tappan has edited out of his columns and then fleshed out and updated. There's something here for everyone. You can't possibly agree with everything you'll find in these pages. Nobody could. But if you're smart, you'll pay attention. Take Mel seriously, and when you don't agree you'll still learn a lot about why you think what you do. And watch out. He might talk you out of your favorite prejudice . . .

Studio City, CA
October, 1981

EDITOR'S PREFACE

Before his unexpected death on November 2, 1980, Mel had planned to revise and expand his *Soldier of Fortune* and *Guns & Ammo* columns in response to thousands of requests from readers. Because of the space limitations imposed by the column format, he felt that much of what he had written was superficial and had planned to write an exhaustive study of long-term survival. With his scholar's passion for exploring all aspects of a subject, the result would have been, not one slim volume such as this, but a 400 page book on each of the chapter headings.

I have chosen to let the columns stand as he wrote them and have only updated information and grouped the material by theme despite the fact that the subjects treated are covered unevenly. Either time ran out before Mel had the chance to write more on a topic, such as medicine, money, barter or the management of stress or, as in the case of firearms, he wrote what may seem to some an inordinate amount because that was the subject in which his readers voiced the greatest interest.

In my opinion, these columns are as important for what they reveal about the man and his approach to problem solving as they are for what they say about long-term survival. As Mel wrote on page 124, "Most problems resolve themselves into self-evident solutions if you have enough reliable information and if you can eliminate emotion from the evaluation of it." Every problem that he encountered he approached with this attitude—be it field stripping a new gun for the first time, analyzing one of his favorite lyric poems or helping a friend in trouble. This method worked for him because he let neither pomposity nor pedantry warp his judgement; he was kind when the easy answer for someone with such quick wit would have been sarcasm and flippancy; and even when confronted with severe physical problems, he never lost the irreverent sense of humor that reminded him and those of us around him that we were, after all, merely human—flawed, funny creatures, but creatures with a brain.

Running like a leitmotif through everything Mel wrote is this theme: Take control of your life by becoming as independent of the system and others as possible and as a first step toward achieving this, learn to look at reality in a hard, unblinking way. Whether he was discussing the .223 cartridge, two-way radio or the economy the underlying message was always the same. I trust that you will see its inherent wisdom.

For 22½ years Mel enriched my life. May this book do the same for yours.

Nancy Tappan
Rogue River, OR
October, 1981

TAPPAN ON SURVIVAL

"Turning and turning in the widening gyre
The falcon cannot hear the falconer;
Things fall apart; the centre cannot hold;
Mere anarchy is loosed upon the world,
The blood-dimmed tide is loosed, . . ."

W.B. Yeats

"Make preparations in advance . . . You
never have trouble if you are prepared
for it."

Theodore Roosevelt

1.

WHY PREPARE?

We are about to witness the profound disruption of this country and, possibly, the entire civilized world. Barring some *deus ex machina* miracle, there is no longer any practical way to prevent it and, unless you are willing to believe or to determine for yourself that what I am telling you here is the truth, you will very probably become a victim of this holocaust without ever having the opportunity to strike a blow on behalf of your country or yourself.

It doesn't take genius to realize that something is wrong. You are paying $7,000 for a $3,000 car, $75,000 for a $20,000 crackerbox tract house, $300 for a no-frills service autopistol and almost $20 for a box of .45 cartridges with which to load it. Major cities and public corporations are being kept from bankruptcy by your tax dollars, whether you like it or not, and most of our leading international banks are insolvent by every standard except the name because of improvident long-term loans to Third World countries, backed by fractional short-term deposits of Arab and other foreign funds subject to sudden withdrawal.

Militarily, our nation has become so weak that when Soviet combat troops are found stationed in Cuba, only 90 miles from our shores, and their presence is officially declared "unacceptable," we then merely accept the situation without action or even further comment. Our stern response to blatant Soviet adventurism in Afghanistan is to withhold our Olympic team from international competition. We have rejected the technological advances that might have brought us parity with our adversaries, such as the neutron bomb and the B-1 bomber, and we have made no effort even to keep our conventional weapons current or at strength. We are completely without practical defenses against nuclear attack, although an effective ABM system is well within our competence, because our leaders fear that even such a clearly passive posture may be perceived as "provocative" by Moscow.[1]

To round out the picture, you may want to recall that the Federal Government is presently spending more of your money on public education than ever before, yet increasing numbers of high school graduates are functionally illiterate. There are more government social programs paying more benefits to more people than at any time in history, yet the recipients' demands are escalating and so is the level of violence with which these demands are underlined. Crime, especially violent crime, is setting new records and we are just beginning to see terrorism expand in this country as it has in Europe.

However unsatisfactory our present national status may be—and it is considerably worse than this brief recital may indicate—it is obviously tolerable. More Americans have enough food on their tables, the telephones work, there are no riots in the streets—except occasionally— over 90 percent of the work force is employed and there is

---

[1]Mel wrote this in August, 1980. Obviously, President Reagan intends to strengthen our defenses; how successful he will be remains to be seen.

still a measure of individual freedom here that surpasses that of any other nation on earth. The nature of our malaise, however, is not static and our condition is on the verge of becoming critical.

Either by sinister design or incredible stupidity, the fools and scoundrels we have elected to represent us in government have debauched our currency, crippled our economy and driven us to bankruptcy. As if that weren't enough, they have created a vast army of bureaucrats— unelected and virtually untouchable—to implement their will: a faceless horde that can create rules with the force of law simply by recording them in the Federal Register. It is through this means that government has reached into almost every phase of our private and professional lives to interfere in ways that elected officials would never dare to do directly, and it is through this means that the vigorous free market which built this country has become so fettered that it will not be able to save us from the impact of more than 40 years of unwise government social engineering and economic meddling.

Do I mean to imply by these observations that the economic, military and social symptoms outlined earlier all arise from the same malady and that its primary cause is government economic interference? Most emphatically, yes, I do.

Since 14 November 1979, we have been under a state of national emergency declared by the President pursuant to the International Emergency Powers Act of 1977. Almost no one seems aware of that fact or of the awesome implications which it carries. By the provisions of this act and its companion legislation entitled Executive Order 11490, the Oval Office is granted sweeping dictatorial powers which virtually suspend all Constitutional safeguards, allow the disbanding of Congress, the freezing of all bank accounts and personal assets, the collection and rationing of all vital commodities, including food, the suspension of passports, full control of the media and private means of communication, including amateur and CB radios, the banning of all travel, public assembly or protest—merely by the stroke of a pen and subject to the approval of no other authority except Congressional review at intervals of six months. (Note Well: On 14 May 1980, Congress reviewed and failed to disapprove the extension of the state of emergency with all attendant powers.)[2]

The ostensible purpose for invoking all of this enormous power was to enable the President to freeze Iranian assets held by U.S. banks in the wake of the terrorist takeover of our embassy in Tehran. I find that curious in view of the fact that at least four other legal avenues—all less cumbersome—were already available to accomplish that simple expedient. A brief order to the Attorney General would have served, for example, and yet the President chose to declare a state of national emergency and to invoke specifically the full range of draconian domestic powers available to him only under those circumstances.

If a chill has not yet begun to ascend your spine, I suggest that you confirm this information for yourself by requesting copies of the legislation from your congressman. The full text is far more ominous than space permits me to indicate here.

Now, this action on the part of the President might look more like personal bravado than serious preparation to deal with the massive civil unrest following from a monetary collapse if it were an isolated incident. It is not. While you are ordering documents from your congressman, ask for a copy of Public Law 96-221. The only mention I have seen of this legislation in the public press indicates that it was designed as a boon to savers, allowing them to receive more interest on their accounts through the gradual elimination of Regulation "Q" restrictions.[3]

---

[2] As of October 3, 1981, we are still in a state of national emergency.
[3] Public Law 96-221 gave us NOW accounts.

In fact, it does a number of far more significant things as well. It frees billions of dollars for lending by the banks that would otherwise have been held as reserves, further fueling inflation, and for the first time it allows the Federal Reserve to print unlimited quantities of Federal Reserve notes (paper money) and to store them for immediate distribution. It increases deposit insurance from $40,000 to $100,000 (reducing the reserves backing up that insurance to about $1.11 for every $100 in deposits), and it empowers the Comptroller of the Currency to proclaim "bank holidays" on a local basis.

A pending bill, S.2305, would require intaglio printing (engraving) on only one side of the dollar bill, allowing at least a 30-percent increase in the production of $5s, $10s, $20s, and $100s. Also pending is H.R. 5961[4], which is being sold to the public by the press as a "drug trafficking" bill, yet it never mentions drugs or drug trafficking. What it does do is to authorize, for the first time in our history, warrantless searches of persons, vehicles and mail leaving the country. It would make cash and monetary instruments equivalent to contraband and it would set up an informer program encouraging citizens to spy on other citizens for rewards of up to $250,000. It would do nothing to control drug trafficking.

To grasp the full impact of what these laws collectively portend, you must have a clear understanding of the nature of inflation and how it works. It is not, as the government and press would have you believe, rising prices. And it is not caused by big business, labor unions or OPEC. Inflation is simply an increase in the supply of money without a commensurate increase in the wealth that backs it. Only governments and, to a lesser degree, lending institutions can create it and only they can stop it.

To be sure, prices rise against an inflated currency, but

[4]These two bills were defeated in the 96th Congress thanks to vigorous outcries from constituents; S.2305, however, has been re-introduced in the 97th Congress as H.R. 4628.

only because the value of that currency is declining through dilution. If you owned an ounce of gold and issued 10 pieces of paper currency against it, each piece would obviously be worth only half as much if you later issued 10 more against the same ounce of gold. Once your butcher or tailor understood that you issued 10 more pieces of paper money against that same ounce of gold every week, his prices to you would increase accordingly until, finally, your paper would have so little value that he would not accept it at all.

An ounce of gold will still buy about the same number of barrels of oil from the OPEC nations as it would when the price of crude was pegged at $2.30 per barrel, but it now takes $35 in paper currency to purchase one barrel. The same relationship holds true domestically as well. Around the turn of the century a $20 gold piece would get you a Colt Single Action or the best ready-made suit on the rack. It still will, but $20 in greenbacks will hardly buy the tie or box of cartridges that used to be thrown in with either transaction.

A look in your wallet will show you why. Notice that all of your bills read "Federal Reserve Note" not "Silver Certificate" as they once did. Our present currency is backed by nothing and convertible into nothing else, much less, "lawful money" as defined by the Constitution. It only has value so long as, and to the degree that, someone is willing to accept it. Were it not for the fact that many other Western nations use the dollar as their reserve currency and have, therefore, a stake in keeping alive the illusion that it has some worth, the U.S. dollar would long since have been allowed to collapse into utter oblivion.

The time is soon coming, however, when we will hyperinflate to such a degree that no one can bail out the dollar. Inflation is almost as old as government itself, but nowhere has the potential for hyperinflation existed that could equal the present situation of the U.S. Government. The Romans under Diocletian inflated by clipping coins and adulterating precious metals with base and the Empire fell. Germany hyperinflated after World War I and accepted Adolph Hitler as an alternative to continuing chaos. (At the height of the Weimar inflation currency was being produced so rapidly that only one side of the bills was printed. Remind you of anything you've read recently?)

At the library or from the U.S. Government Printing Office, get a copy of the "Statement of Liabilities and Other Financial Commitments of the U.S. Government" published by the Treasury Department. On the first page you will see the national debt represented at $650 billion dollars plus—bad enough, since that represents more money than there is—but as you page through the document you will quickly see that this gargantuan sum is only our funded debt: the amount represented by notes and bonds that we are paying interest on.

A little quick arithmetic will indicate that this interest burden alone will soon consume the entire income of the Government from taxes and fees. Just keeping the doors open without budgetary increases requires another one billion a day. And where is that excess to come from? Where all our government deficit spending always has: *they* will simply print some more money and inflate the money supply. The real shock remains. Wait until you total up all of the admitted liabilities—things like Government pension plans, loan guarantees, FHA, veterans' benefits, bank insurance commitments, Social Security and the like. The total is more than *$6 trillion*, and two CPAs I have consulted believe that this figure is *grossly understated.*

Suffice it to say that we owe more than 20 times the money supply and several times our total wealth, both public and private. And we haven't even started bailing out the banks yet! There is no example in history of any nation coming anywhere near this level of debt without a collapse of the entire economy and repudiation or hyperinflation.

Although it may now be too late to stop a socio-economic

collapse from occurring in this country, it is not too late for aware individuals to take independent action to avoid or attenuate its impact upon themselves and those for whom they care. The key to survival preparedness is learning to become, primarily or alternatively, independent of the system. As Teddy Roosevelt observed, "You never have trouble if you are prepared for it." Very soon now, I believe we will have the opportunity to test the wisdom of that dictum. I hope you will join me in the adventure.

When the Nazi regime came to power in the aftermath of Germany's post-WWI hyperinflation, the majority welcomed the stern hand of control and the promised "reform" of monetary excesses. Restrictions on personal freedom were accepted as the price of establishing "order." When strict gun control was instituted early in the first month of the new government's reign, most citizens dutifully complied, turning in even heirlooms and hunting arms.

A few thoughtful individuals who had done their homework on the origins of the National Socialist German Worker's Party and its leader, Adolf Hitler, immediately and quietly made preparations to leave Germany. Their acquaintances and associates derided them openly for overreacting and pointed out the sacrifices which many of them would be making in terms of their finances and careers. The few who withstood the pressure and acted immediately certainly experienced some temporary setbacks, but they escaped with their lives, their families and most of their personal property intact. Some, even those who would later be branded "restricted races," were able to sell their real property and take the proceeds with them.

At each successive stage of repression—when the Jews were made to wear identifying armbands, when their property was confiscated, when they were herded into ghettos and, finally, into concentration camps—a few more understood what was happening and took action to escape the worst of the holocaust, but as the end grew nearer and more obvious, avoiding it became more costly and less certain. And there were always the voices of the imperceptive majority droning the catch phrases that it substitutes for thought: "It couldn't happen here," "It can't get much worse," "World opinion will never permit it," "Sooner or later the government will do something."

This—let us not forget—duly elected and legally constituted government certainly did do something. It murdered a few million of its citizens or, as the enabling laws of the period put it, "terminated certain disruptive social elements" in the interest of "order and the public good." (Note: Tappan's universal rule of law: "The nobler the language, the more nefarious the purpose of any legal instrument.")

There are a number of points valuable to the potential survivalist now that can be drawn from this narrative of the German experience: 1) Independent informed thought, free from current popular opinion, is necessary to perceive the threat, especially at an early stage. 2) Independent action to avoid the consequences of the threat is the only safe course to follow, because the majority seldom recognizes the true nature of a problem until it is too late. 3) Do not rely on the popular press, the authorities or other official sources to warn you or to offer solutions. They are usually part of the problem. 4) The sooner you recognize the threat and begin to prepare, the better your chances for survival.

However instructive the parallels between the German experience of the '20s and '30s and our own present situation, argument by analogy is seldom the most convincing. That is especially true when the topic under discussion is a matter of life or death, entirely outside one's personal experience, and requires that rather far-reaching action be taken before the need for it becomes readily apparent.

In last month's column, I tried to present a comprehensive view of the coming crisis, together with enough corroborating evidence to persuade the perceptive and to provide at least a point of departure for the more skeptical. For a rather detailed analysis of the problem, you may want to read *How to Survive and Prosper in the Next American Depression, War or Revolution* published by Financial Management Associates, 3928 Iowa St., San Diego, CA 92104. I certainly do not agree with many of the conclusions in this volume, but the examination of how we arrived at the brink is well done and the entire book is provocative.

If you have a college level understanding of economics, all you may need to satisfy yourself is a few hours in a library with a copy of this book, indices to the *New York Times*, the *Wall Street Journal* and the *Congressional Record*. If you know what to look for and you are diligent in your research, you will find abundant evidence that 1) a monetary collapse is imminent, 2) the government knows that such a disaster is impending and is preparing to impose draconian measures to enforce its view of order on the population when the event arrives.

Until recently, a good deal of specialized knowledge, an inside information source or two and, perhaps, an act of faith were necessary in order to reach this conclusion with sufficient certainty to make survival preparations a priority concern. There was then, however, ample time to prepare.

Now, we have reached a watershed. Now, for the first time, there is enough unclassified information available supporting this view so that no one who examines enough of the data objectively could remain in doubt. There may yet be time enough to prepare, but I wouldn't care to waste even a day.

If we can agree that serious trouble lies ahead and that the time to make serious preparations to deal with it has arrived, the question remains, "prepare for what?"

It is not possible, obviously, to determine precisely what

course present economic trends will take, how, exactly, the crisis itself will occur or what its aftermath may engender, but there are three likely scenarios that embody among them the most significant elements that are apt to be present.

I. *The classic socio-economic collapse.* Here there is usually a triggering event, causing the various monetary and economic factors which have been in place for some time to become suddenly manifest. Any of the following would serve as catalyst and there are many more that would do as well: refusal by OPEC or the Common Market nations to accept the dollar in exchange for goods, a terrorist-inspired nuclear explosion in either New York City, Los Angeles or Washington, D.C., a *major* earthquake in California, a decision by a major industrial country to exclude the dollar as reserve currency, a transportation strike during the winter coupled with almost any other national crisis.

Massive violence, rioting and looting would erupt—at least in the cities. Food and other essentials would be exhausted in less than a week and arson would be the probable response to empty shelves. Firestorms would soon sweep every major city. Water and sanitation would fail, disease would become rampant, and survivors would begin scouring the countryside in search of food, shelter and valuables.

Small towns, especially rural small towns not too close to the cities, should fare much better. The central government would probably fall and, depending upon the length of the crisis period, communities might form into alliances resembling city states. Loss of life would probably be very high and a long period of anarchy would probably exist before successful attempts at rebuilding could be made.

Preparations for this contingency are necessarily extensive but relatively uncomplicated. Given the right location and skills, careful planning and the means to provide almost total self-sufficiency, even a worst-case version of this scenario could be weathered—not only safely but with some comfort.

Most survivalists seem to favor some version of this general theme. It is certainly the most straightforward unravelling of our complex economic ills, but it may not be the most likely.

Please note that I did not term this scenario "unlikely." It may very well be the first to occur, but I do want to point out that preparing solely for this contingency is shortsighted, since it will only happen if a crisis develops virtually overnight in response to a precipitating occurrence: e.g., a public repudiation by the Soviet bloc of the $70 billion-plus borrowed from U.S. lending institutions, causing rampant bank failures to develop more quickly than the government can intervene.

If there is no triggering event, no sudden dramatic climax to stimulate a simultaneous eruption of problems so massive as to overwhelm the legislative machinery created to deal with them, then we may encounter a very different denouement indeed.

II. Dictatorship—Police State. In the absence of one crisis potentiating the effect of another, our various economic time bombs will tend to manifest themselves seriatim and, on that basis, the government can cope with them for a protracted period. Even though it cannot solve the problem, it has the power to apply band-aids and then go on to the next crisis.

For example, when inflation reaches levels just short of initiating public rioting, wage and price controls will be instituted. Never mind that they will create essential shortages and a black-market economy—Big Brother will deal with that problem when *it* surfaces. Next may be a liquidity crunch and bank runs. The machinery is already in place to declare a "temporary" moratorium on loans and to supply unlimited printing-press currency to the banks without collateral and without regard to their financial condition. (Why not? The stuff they are printing isn't really money.)

The stunning inflation that will result may then be defused by another delaying tactic, and all the while a steady stream of propaganda will be explaining away these "extraordinary," "temporary" occurrences, and new controls, rules and restraints will be put into place as rapidly as they can be distributed. All of these will be for "the public good" and against the makers of "obscene profits."

Do not underestimate the government's power to intervene. It may lack the ability ultimately to prevent a monetary collapse, but it might well be able to orchestrate the aftermath. After all, our leaders know that a crisis is coming, and specific legislation for dealing with bank runs, exceptional currency requirements and civil disorders is—as I pointed out last month—either in place or pending.

Further, when the trouble starts, most people will not understand what is happening, nor will they know that their daily burgeoning problems—such as buying food and other essentials, losing their jobs and increased incidence of street violence—are government-caused. Instead, out of fear, they will believe whatever line of propaganda the government chooses to feed them, and they will actually call for and welcome the most stringent government controls.

The key to whether a dictatorship and a police state emerge from this chaos is the military. Will the armed forces and National Guard remain essentially intact to enforce the will of the government against fellow citizens? Some might continue because they believe such action would be in their self-interest. Even though money were worthless and they couldn't be paid conventionally, some sort of priority script would probably be issued, and the military would certainly be in a position to confiscate all known food supplies.

Even larger numbers might remain loyal to the

government out of a misguided sense of patriotism—a tendency to confuse one's country with its government. If a soldier doesn't understand the background of the collapse, is not expecting it and only confusion and chaos seem to prevail outside the gates of his base, simply obeying orders may appear the safest course to follow.

In many ways, this second scenario is the most difficult for which to prepare and the one which offers the least chance of surviving the disaster completely unscathed.

III. War. Two years ago I would have said that war or the threat of war as international blackmail was the least likely of the three primary scenarios. After all, why wouldn't the Soviets merely outlast us? Politically and militarily things are certainly going their way, thanks in no small measure to some incredibly stupid moves on our part—such as no-win war policies, gigantic loans and food shipments—allowing them both to feed their people *and* to outspend us on defense.

That logic no longer obtains, however. The Soviet economy is presently in even worse condition than our own, and by 1982 the Russians will be net importers of oil. Internally, their condition is desperate—and a new element has been added. They now have contempt for U.S. willingness to protect its own vital interests, and that attitude, coupled with their pressing need for oil, may well lead to further Soviet adventurism and a serious confrontation which neither side wants. Since both we and they have now adopted counterforce targeting, it is conceivable that either side may believe a limited nuclear exchange to be feasible.

Far more probable, however, are the prospects that emerge from the Soviet development of Directed Energy Weapons, specifically High Energy Lasers and the Particle Beam Generator. Former Air Force Intelligence Chief General Keegan believes that the Particle Beam device will be fully deployed in the Soviet Union by the end of 1981, and information I have developed independently suggests a time frame as early as April.

This device, which accelerates subatomic particles to the speed of light, in effect throws a lightning bolt as large as 200 miles in diameter, and it has the ability to alter the molecular structure of its target. No more than six, properly located, would make the entire Soviet Union completely invulnerable to attack by ICBMs or conventional aircraft.

The day after these were deployed, the President of the United States might be informed by hot line and invited to take his best shot at Moscow for proof. Within a week new "trade and exchange" agreements could be ratified by Congress and a new era of peace and cooperation would be ushered in without a shot being fired. It could be years before anyone even knew what happened and by then . . .

Finally, don't overlook the possibility that we have people in our government who are perfectly capable of starting a hot war if things get too far out of hand domestically, in order to unite the nation against a common enemy and to delay the coming economic chaos.

The one thing which each of these scenarios demands is taking immediate action to the end of becoming prepared to live self-sufficiently away from urban centers and independent of the present economic system. Your first concerns should be with the means of providing security, food and water, proper location and health care.

QUESTIONS & ANSWERS

Q: I know things look bad economically now but do you really think we could have national disaster like you write about? I think the government will stop it before it happens. When the truth finally comes out, I think everybody will see that it's the oil companies that are causing all this inflation. I hope we do tax their obscene windfall profits and if they don't straighten out, I think we ought to nationalize them. C.R., OK

A: First, let's all understand the term "inflation." It does not mean high or rising prices. Inflation is simply an increase in the money supply without a concomitant and equal increase in the wealth that backs that money supply. It is true that when you print more dollars, the result is usually that prices will increase because each piece of paper that is reputed to be a "dollar" is actually worth less each time the number of them is increased. For example, if you owned a pound of gold and decided to issue ten paper shares in it, each would represent a tenth of a pound of gold. If the local merchants accepted these pieces of paper in payment for goods, a "price" in these shares would be established. If you issued another ten pieces of paper (now each piece is worth only 1/20 of a pound of gold), it wouldn't be long before prices doubled.

It is important that you see the distinction between inflation and high prices because any number of things can cause prices to rise, but only the government can cause inflation because only the government prints money. It isn't about to stop, and nothing else—short of a war—could possibly prevent an overwhelming economic upheaval from occurring in the fairly near future.

Now I hold no particular brief for the oil companies, but their slice of your gasoline dollar is already piddling compared to the portion that goes for taxes. The breakdown goes like this:

Producing country $0.49
Oil Company costs (transportation, refining, etc.).. .16
Oil Company profits .... .04
Local service station gross (before expenses) ...... .13
Taxes .... .18
$1.00

Profits are not obscene. People working to benefit themselves have made this the greatest nation on earth. What we need to worry about is obscene government.

Q: I have been reading your columns since they first started and I'll admit they've shaken me up. I also think you are sincere in your beliefs, but don't you think things are getting better lately? The government says that if we all do our part we can lick inflation and I think we can if big business would hold prices down and we got a good energy program. I also read where we are going to support the dollar to keep it from falling any more on the international markets. K.M., VA

A: Much as I dislike being cast in a negative role, I must disagree with you entirely. Having the government urge us, as private citizens, to fight inflation is like having an airline pilot tell the passengers that the plane is going too fast and suggesting that they all stick their heads out of a window and blow. You and I are not the cause of inflation and neither is industry or labor. Prices and wages increase to compensate for the dollar's declining value. Only the issuer of money—in our case, the government—can debase it by issuing so many vouchers (paper dollars) that they become worthless.

Goods and services are no more expensive in terms of real money (gold) than they have ever been. They only seem so because our currency is becoming valueless. For example, around the turn of the century a $20 U.S. gold piece would buy a new Colt Single Action revolver, or the best ready made suit of clothes on the rack. It still will, but a $20 Federal Reserve Note won't.

Don't be misled by attempts to shift the blame to the "energy crisis," "big business," labor unions or the fact that your wife uses imported perfume. The problem is simple, though the solution is not; our government prints increasing amounts of currency and dumps it into the economy by spending, without ever creating a single penny of wealth. That is why the dollar is daily becoming more nearly worthless—both absolutely and in relation to other, more stable currencies.

19

2.

SURVIVAL CHECKLIST

Over the past few months, the mail has brought repeated requests for some sort of checklist that could be applied to one's personal preparedness program. The subject is obviously too complex for any such list to be comprehensive without a great deal of elaboration, specialized knowledge and, probably, personal counsel, but—used prudently—such an inventory could provide an overview of what I'm trying to accomplish in these columns and give those of you who are serious about preparing an outline on which you can begin to build for yourselves.

The kind of disaster that you expect to occur is going to affect the way in which you adapt this outline to your personal needs. I have drawn it with a monetary collapse in mind, since the odds presently favor that event by a substantial margin. If you see nothing more than a severe inflationary recession, you may want to eliminate or reduce the emphasis on several points. On the other hand, if you foresee a nuclear confrontation as an adjunct to the economic chaos, there are several additional categories which you will need to consider. Finally, these recommendations reflect my own judgements; your personal circumstances may well change some of the priorities as I have set them down. If you think that you should buy some coins before you get into trade goods, we have no quarrel. I do think, however, that the first seven items on the list are all "priority one" and should be pursued concurrently, to the extent possible.

1. YOU.

The most important factor in the survival equation is you: your physical health and your cast of mind—particularly the way in which you handle stress. However you feel and whatever state of health you *think* you enjoy, get a *complete* physical from your doctor. Find out your exercise tolerance, lung capacity, cholesterol and triglyceride levels, blood pressure, and ask at the beginning to have your blood typed. You should be comfortable enough with your physician to discuss your survival concerns frankly, otherwise he might not order all the tests you should have. For example, if there were no indications to suggest it he might —quite properly—omit a glucose tolerance test unless you told him that you expected to change your diet radically, living on nothing but stored foods or foraging. If you can't be completely frank with him or if you are otherwise dissatisfied with your physician, now is the time to look for another. In addition to your check-up, you are going to need his help for a number of other things, including the development of a suitable fitness program and, possibly, helping you to acquire portions of your medical kit as well as some hard-to-come-by important medical books.

If you need minor elective surgery, get it out of the way as soon as possible and discuss with your doctor the advisability of prophylactic surgery such as having your appendix removed. There are some serious pros and cons to be considered in that connection and you will need competent medical advice from someone who shares—or at least understands—your survival concerns.

You should also see an eye specialist who can assess the health of your eyes as well as insure that you are properly fitted with glasses, if you need them. Obviously, if corrective lenses are prescribed, you should buy several pair *in practical frames* and, if your prescription is changed, save your old lenses. They could be better than nothing in an emergency.

Teeth too should get their share of scrutiny. If you are 47 and still waiting for those last two wisdom teeth to descend, give up the hope and have them out now so that your wife won't have to do the job some evening by candlelight with a razor blade and a pair of vise grip pliers.

Once you know the present state of your health, you should begin to do what you can to improve it. With your physician, work out a reasonable, interesting (so that you will stick to it) exercise program designed to increase your stamina and capacity for sustained physical work. Neither tennis nor golf will do. You need something that will create a steady muscular demand and increase your heart and respiration rate (your personal health permitting) for at least a half hour per day, *everyday.*

Stop smoking or, at least, inhaling. If you inhale tobacco smoke, you now have some degree of *permanent* lung damage. Further, if you are hooked on tobacco—or anything else—your options under survival conditions are reduced.

Adjust your weight to a sensible level. If you are more than 25 pounds over or under your ideal weight, bring it in line by adopting sensible eating habits. No fad diets, please; just better nutrition and an adjustment of quantity. Along with heredity, not inhaling tobacco smoke and controlling your blood pressure, many physicians believe that optimal weight maintenance is one of the leading factors in preventing heart attacks and cardio-vascular accidents.

If you have more than three alcoholic drinks of any kind or if you consume more than four ounces of whiskey (or its equivalent) per day, seek the counsel of your doctor. Current literature indicates that regular alcoholic intake in excess of those figures causes marked changes in the cardio-vascular system. It should go without saying that the so-called "recreational use" of drugs has no place in survival preparedness.

Discuss with your medical advisor the management of any chronic illnesses you have, in detail. Buy your prescription drugs in quantity and rotate them to keep fresh supplies on hand. Find out if there are substitutes for the drugs you must take or if they could be eliminated entirely by another course of treatment. For example, if you are diabetic and taking insulin, inquire whether an oral preparation with longer shelf life could be substituted or whether, in your. particular case, strict diet control measures could be made to suffice.

Once you have embarked on a program to improve your physical health, you may want to give some thought to what the current vernacular might term "where your head is at." How you react to stress, your personal hang-ups, the way in which you interact with other people—these factors, perhaps more than anything else, are likely to determine whether you survive a crisis. There are tests that you can take to determine how successfully you cope with reality, but, except in rare circumstances, you probably don't need to take them. Unless you are seriously mentally ill—and sometimes even then—you can see your own mental shortcomings, if you are willing to undergo the rather painful experience. Sitting alone, quietly in a room, completely without distractions for, perhaps, half an hour, will allow you to observe many of your own mental processes as well as much of the distracting "chatter" that goes on constantly in your mind. For more information in this area, you might begin by reading Robert Ornstein's book, *The Psychology of Consciousness,* and contacting The Foundation of Human Understanding (P.O. Box 34036, Los Angeles, CA 90034) for free information about a simple mental observation technique that can teach you to maintain control of your emotions in the face of extreme pressure.

2. DEVELOP NECESSARY SKILLS.

Next to physical and mental health, the most important consideration for the aspiring survivalist is the development of vital skills. Make a list of what you consider the minimum number of skills that you would need to keep yourself and your family alive over a protracted period with no outside help and start learning them at once. Then, if time permits, make another, including areas of expertise that are desirable, if not essential, and so on. At a minimum, your basic list should include emergency medical care, hunting and foraging for food, *practical* defensive shooting, *practical* unarmed combat, basic woodscraft, using tools and making essential repairs to your shelter, firearms and other indispensable items. If your present job seems an unlikely profession after the collapse, you may also want to consider learning a new trade that is almost certain to be in demand, such as construction, mechanical repair or the like.

You will need to learn quite a bit more in some of these areas than others. In the case of medical care, for example, mastering a simple first aid course will probably not be enough. In some areas citizens are allowed, if not encouraged, to take the courses offered for paramedics. If it's possible for you, by all means do it; if not, at least go through the advanced Red Cross course and take a separate one in CPR from a qualified instructor. Whatever you do, get a Dorland's *Medical Encyclopedia* and a Gray's *Anatomy* to learn the vocabulary of medicine and the basics of how the body functions and is constructed. Without these you'll have a hard time understanding the other medical books you should have. I recommend about 20 such volumes to my clients, but at the very least you should have: the latest *Merck Manual* (currently the 13th edition), *Emergency Treatment and Management* by T. Flint and H.D. Cain, *Management of Medical Emergencies* (2nd edition) by

J.C. Sharpe and F. Marx, *Manual of Medical Therapeutics* (22nd edition), Washington University School of Medicine (eds. Costrini and Thompson), *Cutting's Handbook of Pharmacology* (5th edition) and *Fundamental Skills in Surgery* (2nd edition) by T.F. Nealon. (I'm not suggesting that you indulge in do-it-yourself brain surgery, but this is a handy, simple source book should you ever be forced to suture a wound or amputate a gangrenous toe.) A *PDR* or *Physician's Desk Reference* is also extremely useful.

Hunting and foraging are skills that most readers of *Guns & Ammo* probably possess to some degree, but don't neglect trapping, calling, baiting, and jacklighting as well as other techniques that may be illegal and unsportsmanlike now, but essential in an emergency. For a complete catalog on calling supplies you might try: Burnham Brothers (P.O. Box 78, Marble Falls, OK 78654). Also, be sure that you learn to distinguish the more common edible plants in your retreat area and *all* of the poisonous ones.

You will note that I have emphasized the word "practical" as applied to defensive shooting and unarmed combat. A hunter safety course is not equivalent to the basic training available at Jeff Cooper's GUNSITE Ranch (Box 401, Paulden, AZ 86334) and winning a black belt in sport karate is probably not going to be as useful as learning a half dozen simple but decisive moves well enough to make them reflexive.

You probably know whether you need martial arts training, but gun buffs often delude themselves about their shooting ability—particularly their prowess as combat pistoleros. If you're serious enough about survival to want to know the truth, let me suggest a simple, but revealing test. Find a safe place to shoot without too many curious onlookers and bring a friend with you. Set up a silhouette target or simply a 24-inch wide x 36-inch long sheet of wrapping paper at a *measured* 25 yards. Then with your friend timing you and blowing a start and stop signal on a loud whistle at five-second intervals, draw your pistol of choice (in a serious caliber) and fire five shots at the center of the target mass, within the allotted five seconds. Reload and repeat. If all of your shots can be contained within a 10-inch circle four times out of five, your survival index is probably adequate. If not, you need training. (Unless you are *well practiced*, never attempt a speed draw with live ammo. Start with your gun in your hand by your side, well away from your body.)

3. START COLLECTING REFERENCE MATERIALS.

Books and magazine articles on practical subjects will be among your most valuable survival assets. Obviously, "how to" books in a variety of fields are a must, especially construction, repair, farming, trapping, raising animals, cooking game, making clothing, leather and woodworking, reloading, making tools and the like. Don't forget homely topics such as repairing water pumps and cleaning septic tanks. Make certain that you buy the shop manuals published by the manufacturer for repairing each of your cars or trucks.

Be sure to include as many books as you can that emphasize the use of hand tools and simple techniques. The *Foxfire Books* and similar volumes which offer more primitive alternatives to elaborate modern technology are especially useful.

In addition to expanding your range of essential skills, your survival library should also provide entertainment as well as the means of educating your children and stimulating your own intellectual growth. If you need help in this area, a good place to begin is the *Reader's Advisor*, available in the reference room of most libraries.

General reference books are also virtually indispensable. At the very least you should have the latest *World Almanac*, an authoritative dictionary such as the large *Webster's International* (2nd or 3rd) unabridged, the *American Heritage* or the *Webster's New World*. A quality encyclopedia such as the new *Britannica III* could be worth its weight in gold, but even a one-volume, desk edition such as the *Columbia* will prove highly useful. For more suggestions on general reference books, you might begin by consulting Constance Winchell's *A Guide to Reference Books* in your public library. It would require several times the space we have here just to list all of the topics you should consider including in your survival library, and still there would be no room to mention specific titles. Let me suggest, therefore, the following sources to get you started. Survival, Inc. (17019 Kingsview, Carson, CA 90746) has a booklist in its catalog ($2) and they sell *Survival Books 1981*, an annotated bibliography, for $14.95. Loompanics, Inc. (P.O. Box 264, Mason, MI 48854) offers an interesting catalog for $3 emphasizing books on various aspects of self-sufficiency and maximizing personal freedom and Earthbooks Lending Library (Box 556, Harmony, PA 16037) provides a unique rental-purchase option plan for survival oriented books. This concern offers a unique service, so far as I know. You can rent any book they carry (an extensive list) for a modest fee and either return it or buy it at a discount. Catalog $1.00.

Some portion of your budget should be set aside for essential periodicals. You will probably find a complete file of *Mother Earth News* helpful. Kurt Saxon's *The Survivor* (P.O. Box 327, Harrison, AR 72601) is particularly useful for learning to improvise. He emphasizes 19th century, kitchen-table technology, reprints from long out-of-print sources and his own valuable—often brilliant—insights into the psychology of long-term survival. Bound volumes of back issues are available and, at $11 each or $40 per set they are a bargain.

There are a number of good newsletters currently available such as *Daily News Digest* (P.O. Box 39850, Phoenix, AZ 85069, $150 per year), *The Reaper* (P.O. Box 39026, Phoenix, AZ 85069, $225 per year) and *Remnant Review* (P.O. Box 39800, Phoenix, AZ 85069, $95 per year). For financial preparedness and interpretation of current events, they are all worth reading, particularly so far as timing is concerned. For in-depth information on physical survival by the leading experts in the field, you may want to examine a monthly publication which I edit called *Personal Survival Letter* (P.O. Box 598, Rogue River, OR 97537, $125 per year). It contains definitive articles on such practical survival topics as food storage, survival vehicles and alternative fuel supplies, combat shooting techniques, emergency medicine, establishing a retreat, anti-terrorist tactics, reviews of little-known survival products and detailed comparisons of currently available battle rifles and other defensive arms.

4. GUNS AND AMMO.

With the exception of your own skills and mental preparation, nothing is likely to be more important to your survival than your firearms. In past issues of this column as well as in my book, *Survival Guns*, I have dealt with this topic at some length, so nothing more than a brief word should be necessary here. Please remember, however, that the criteria for selecting arms to be used for sporting purposes are quite different from those that pertain to choosing survival guns. It is especially important that you do not try to make hunting arms substitute for proper defensive weaponry. The reverse is also true, but perhaps to a more limited extent. In some cases, skillful modifications will be in order to make your battery as reliable and efficient as it should be for this demanding use. A well selected inventory of spare parts is a must as is the skill to make basic repairs. Brownell's *Encyclopedia of Modern Firearms, Parts and Assembly* and *Gunsmith Kinks* as well as the NRA *Firearms Assembly I and II* will go a long way toward helping you to keep your guns shooting under adverse conditions.

5. FOOD AND WATER STORAGE.

Anyone who depends on public utilities for his water supply now should have—at a minimum—one week's water ration put up in containers made for the purpose or else in plastic bleach bottles, together with a few drops of chlorine bleach or iodine as a preservative. Small portable water purifiers such as the Water Washer which employ both silver ionization and activated charcoal filtering should be considered an integral part of any storage program. At your retreat, you will, of course, need a well or some other independent, continuing source of water. But even then, water storage should not be neglected because well pumps do break, streams become polluted and springs often fail during droughts.

Food storage is a fairly complicated matter and certainly one of the most vital aspects of survival preparedness. Consequently, it is best undertaken on an individual basis with the help of a knowledgeable expert. Do not, however, settle for any company's prepackaged "one year's supply." Although some are certainly better than others (a few one year's supplies provide only 900-1,100 calories per day and others are filled with cheap calories such as mashed potatoes, corn meal and peas), it makes no more sense to buy your food storage in this manner than it does to have the supermarket bag boy select your weekly groceries. I recommend that your supply—plus vitamin supplements—be designed to meet your own tastes and physical requirements. My own contains a three-month "wet pack" of ordinary canned goods and other super-market foods which we rotate regularly. Then we have another three month's supply consisting largely of compressed freeze-dried foods, which is highly portable and can be made table ready with a minimum of energy. The balance of our storage includes air-dried vegetables and fruit, because we prefer the taste, compactness and price of most produce when prepared by this method. Freeze-dried real meats in considerable quantity and variety round out our program. I doubt the viability of TVP in large quantities as a satisfactory meat substitute and the flavored varieties contain entirely too much salt and preservatives for my taste. Especially prepared vacuum packed salad oil is another essential for any long-term storage program, as is non-instant, non-fat powdered milk. We also like to include quantities of herbs and spices to help make strange edibles more palatable. Curry and chili powder were, after all, peasant inventions to mask unpleasant flavors and aromas of foraged or questionable foods.

This basic program can be extended to, perhaps, double the man/days fairly inexpensively by adding "the basic four" in sufficient quantity: 300 pounds of hard red winter wheat (at least 15 percent protein content), 100 pounds of powdered milk, 100 pounds of honey and 8 pounds of salt. I prefer that all of these items be prepared for storage by one of the better commercial firms and the milk *must* be for reasonable shelf life—but you can save money by packaging some of them yourself.

Practice using storable foods in your daily menus now—later is not the time to learn either their eccentricities or the threshhold of your gag reflex. Some items are delicious and others may take some getting used to, or at least some imaginative preparation. Get as many books as you can on preparing dried foods as well as cooking wild game. Do not rely on the old saw that if you're hungry enough you will eat anything. That has proved to be tragically untrue in documented cases.

Don't forget a hand grinder for the wheat and you may want to include some books and equipment to help preserve the food you grow and hunt for later on. A few vacuum packed cans of assorted garden seed from Survival Inc. (17019 Kingsview, Carson, CA 90746) are also good insurance.

6. RETREATS.

Whether you prefer to call them retreats, refuges, or havens, having a safe place to go—away from the cities—during a major crisis is one of the two most important factors in a realistic program of long-term survival preparedness (the other is having the means of self-protection and food gathering). During the aftermath of a major catastrophe such as a monetary collapse or a nuclear exchange, the cities will contain the greatest concentration of the most desperate, dangerous, systems-dependent people. It would be virtually impossible to have your own well or other independent water supply there; hunting, fishing, and foraging would obviously be out of the question; growing enough food in a garden, even on a large lot, would be difficult at best and just trying it would make you a target. Without utilities, sanitation and a public health service, most cities would become nightmares of disease within a fortnight, and if that weren't enough, the inevitable arson committed by looters and other violence-prone denizens would—without the customary services of the fire department—develop into firestorms, incinerating every structure and creature in the area.

7. TOOLS FOR SELF-SUFFICIENT LIVING.

This category properly includes all of the apparatuses useful or necessary to making your way without outside help—such obvious items as knives, axes and other edged tools; construction and repair implements; farm and garden tools, hunting, fishing and general outdoor gear; communications devices.

8. ALTERNATE ENERGY SOURCES.

This topic can be of great or little concern depending upon your personal retreat plans, requirements and taste. It may be as uncomplicated as substituting wood for whatever you now use for heating and cooking, or as complex as building a solar energy home with wind or hydroelectric power as a backup. Some will want to consider converting their cars or trucks to run on alternate fuels, while others will merely turn to bicycles or horses. A good place to start your research here is with the *Energy Primer* published by the *Whole Earth Catalog* people. It and the

Mother Earth News® Handbook of Homemade Power will lead you to most of the other books on the subject.

9. TRADE GOODS.

Such items as ammunition, fishhooks, knives and needles are likely to be of much greater value for some time after the collapse than any of the traditional forms of money, including gold and silver. **Small, useful, manufactured items such as these which require heavy industrial equipment to fabricate and for which there are** not easily improvised, efficient substitutes should be your first choice. Rimfire ammunition is a good example. Almost everyone owns a .22, and yet there is certainly no reasonably effective kitchen table method of making ammunition for them. The time may well be near when you can exchange a handful of these useful cartridges for a cow, bushels of produce or virtually anything else that you may need.

10. MONEY.

This is another of those topics that will require at least a full column even to approach useful coverage. [1] If you feel that you must do something until that article appears, buy at least one full bag ($1,000 face value) of U.S. silver coins dated 1964 or earlier, having no numismatic value. These are known in the trade as "common date" or "junk" silver coins because they are not rare, but they *do* have the silver content and they *are* recognizable as money. Because of the decline in the value of paper dollars, such honest money will cost you more than three times its face value. Considering the real value of Federal Reserve Notes, however, it is a bargain at the price. In an upcoming column, we will discuss bullion, gold coins, diamonds and other forms of preserving your buying power, but unless you are an expert, stay away from them until then. These are not investments for the uninitiated.

[1]Mel never got to write the column on money but his advice in this short paragraph is still sound.

QUESTIONS & ANSWERS

Q: You and others have convinced me that we are headed for a total monetary collapse and a real upheaval as a result, but don't you think you carry the survival preparations a little too far? The head of a well-known survival newsletter says that guns will not be necessary when the collapse comes because there will not be any violence except in some big cities. He says that if we have a year's supply of food, some gold and silver coins, a home in the suburbs and a wood stove, we will survive O.K., especially if we warn our neighbors to prepare too. Mrs. S.B., TX

A: When you begin to read extensively in survival literature, you will encounter a good deal of conflicting advice and only you can make the final decision of how much to prepare—or, for that matter, whether to prepare at all. None of us can do more than warn you that trouble is coming, give you our reasons for thinking so, and then, if we are skilled, suggest specific ways in which you may reduce your risks from those hazards that might logically be expected to develop as a result of the particular kind of trouble we anticipate.

I prefer to believe that no one professionally engaged in giving advice on life and death matters would deliberately seek to gain popularity by handing out comforting, easy answers to the highly complex and perilous problems that disaster survival poses. But that point of view occasionally leaves me puzzled since, as you say, there are those who accept the premise that a breakdown in the social order is coming—with its attendant loss of essential services, vital food production and distribution—yet they insist that widespread violence will not occur and some even recommend against taking steps to provide for your own protection, if it should. I earnestly hope that they are right and I am wrong, but what if the reverse proves to be true? Holocaust or not, it is utter foolishness for any adult not to own a defensive firearm and the skill to use it to protect himself and his family. Even today, no one can guarantee your safety except you.

3.

RETREATING

The concept most fundamental to realistic long-term disaster preparedness is retreating; having a safe place to go in order to avoid the concentrated violence destined to erupt in the cities—a place where, in addition to owning greater safety during the crisis interval, one can reasonably expect to generate subsistence for an indefinite period thereafter. Despite its central importance to the business of staying alive in the aftermath of a pervasive disaster, such as a monetary collapse or a nuclear exchange, this aspect of the survival equation is not widely understood.

Most people who approach the topic for the first time tend to be hampered by what I call the "backpacker mentality." They tend to conceive of disaster survival in terms of an extended wilderness adventure in which they somehow manage to escape from the cities in the nick of time, just ahead of the fleeing mobs, carrying all they will need for shelter, food, clothing, medical care and protection in a pack on their backs, in the saddle bags of a ten-speed bicycle or in the trunk of the family car. Another common misconception centers around the isolated wilderness cabin or mountain stronghold where a single family or a few friends expect to fend off all comers, in the event of their being discovered.

Now, those of us who see the need to make serious survival preparations have to begin our thinking somewhere, and it's no disgrace to start with these obvious clichés. The danger lies in not thinking beyond them. Unfortunately, the gross inadequacy of current survival literature does not tend to lead one further, because most of it seems to confuse the romance of woodscraft, nomadics and homesteading with the hard realities of disaster survival. The hackneyed retreat alternatives so shallowly conceived and so tirelessly repeated by the few writers on the subject are, upon careful examination, either simplistic, unworkable or of severely limited value in the real world. Some of them have a transient appeal, in a Walter Mitty sort of way, and they can spark some remarkably interesting table conversation. Who among us has never dreamed of sailing off to exotic climes, leaving the humdrum world behind; who doesn't cherish a secret longing for a hideaway back of beyond—a rough hewn cabin snug against the winter, smoke curling from a stone chimney? These things have an archetypical appeal and they are exciting to contemplate—so long as your commitment does not go beyond talking and wool gathering. Only in the rarest circumstances, however, could a thoughtful, practical, reasonably prudent individual be expected to stake his life and that of his family on any of them.

Once you have reached the point where you feel that preparedness is no longer academic, and you have a growing, apprehensive awareness that the time grows short for you to relocate away from the areas of greatest danger, it becomes increasingly easy to see the shortcomings of the traditional retreat alternatives. The sea-going approach, for example, is simply out of the question for more than a minuscule few; the land mobile techniques so widely touted by at least one writer are patently irresponsible; isolated wilderness retreats are virtually indefensible by an average family; group retreats sound good in theory but once you begin investigating actual examples, serious problems become apparent. There are too many rules and regulations, or too few; there is great difficulty in getting a good balance of needed skills in the group since awareness of the need for retreating does not even roughly coincide with a cross section of occupations in a balanced community (too many doctors and lawyers, for example, and not enough plumbers, electricians or carpenters). Further, I am sorry to say, many group retreats appear to be nothing more than promotional schemes, and quite a large number seem to have been set up by persons who might be classified technically as "whacko." Often these communal arrangements make no provision for permanent dwellings of any kind and concern for privacy within the group is customarily given scant attention. Whether utopias or group retreats, artificial communities have a tendency not to work out. Since few, if any, of them allow occupancy now, you would have no way of knowing whether they were viable until the convening of the crisis—and then it would be too late.

To ice the matter, most of these cliché retreat alternatives require crystal ball timing. Because they are generally such an extreme departure from conventional life patterns, one would hardly choose to activate his retreat plan a moment sooner than necessary. Who would willingly elect, before circumstances forced him, to start blundering through the bush for months on end in a flimsy motorhome, popping its staples with every mile, towing a reluctant trailer containing all his possessions? Who would choose to live aboard a cramped sailboat with three kids and a pregnant wife even a week longer than he had to?

Yet those who delay seeking their retreats until the crisis strikes may never reach them.

So much, then, for easy answers. The truth is that establishing and occupying a retreat is serious business. It is going to involve extensive, informed planning tailored to the precise needs of the people who will use it, and the problems which must be resolved in making such an arrangement viable under crisis conditions are enormous. There are also emotional factors involved which other aspects of survival preparation do not engender. It's one thing to buy a gun or two and some storable food; quite another to completely restructure one's entire mode of living. Still, it is far more reasonable to plan the details of a new lifestyle carefully in advance than to be thrust into whatever niche chance may offer when the crisis arrives.

Almost two years ago, my wife and I established a workable retreat, after several false starts and some expensive mistakes. Whether or not you are ready to make the commitment necessary to take that step, I think it is important that you understand why lesser measures will not do.

The truth is that any realistic retreat plan is going to involve a good deal of effort on your part and possibly substantial expense as well as significant rearrangement of your lifestyle. People seldom take such serious steps without a firm commitment, and I believe that you are more likely to reach that point of determination if you arrive at your own idea of what you need by setting up your own list of objective criteria, based on an informed analysis of what the coming holocaust is apt to be like and the functions that a retreat would have to fulfill under those conditions.

Although the criteria you establish should reflect your own personal requirements in the greatest possible detail, there are also a number of objective considerations which must be taken into account because they are common to

40

virtually any catastrophic occurrence having long-term consequences.

One of these is the probability of concerted, widespread violence which may last for a protracted period at a relatively high level. A prominent newsletter pundit urges—for whatever reason—that you take no steps to protect yourself against that eventuality. None of us knows, of course, exactly what will occur, but of all the possible scenarios, unrestrained violence and looting seem the most probable. How anyone could view the power outages in New York City or the strikes of police and firemen in Memphis and elsewhere without reaching that conclusion is simply beyond my ken. It should be obvious that the mass hysteria and unbridled fear stemming from a crisis of the magnitude contemplated here will not have a calming effect upon the hatred and fragmentation that already exist in our society. Further, in addition to the violence prone, there will also be the element of normally decent people who didn't prepare and who will try to take what they need by whatever means necessary to keep themselves and their families alive.

When the food stores are empty, the fires will begin. Arson seems to be one of the commonest accompaniments to riots and it is unreasonable to believe that firemen and police will be reporting for duty to protect your home when they could be fleeing the cities with their families— especially since there will be no money with which to pay them for their services.

Logically, those who have survived the first hours or days of the holocaust in the cities will begin to flee—if they have not already done so—when the public water supply and sanitation facilities fail and disease begins to be a factor. Small, isolated farms will become targets for looters and the hoards pouring out of metropolitan areas will probably converge on known food producing areas, such as the Central Valley of California, for example, or established resorts where it may be presumed that the affluent have vacation homes stocked with food and supplies.

Assuming that you have made reasonable preparations to live self-sufficiently, the greatest single danger to your survival when the crisis strikes will be your proximity to concentrated masses of systems-dependent people. Remaining in a city is totally out of the question and even living in a relatively out of the way place in an area of high overall population density is extremely hazardous. New York State, New England and Pennsylvania, for example, contain some lovely rural sites that might appear suitable for retreats, at first glance, but they could all be overrun by fleeing mobs and bands of looters within hours. A major factor in your location of a retreat, then, ought to be population density. Not only should your chosen site be at least a tank of gasoline away from major metropolitan areas, but the ambient population should be low as well.

Nuclear power plants in the vicinity of your proposed retreat also pose an unnecessary risk. As Paul Ehrlich points out in his book, *The End of Affluence,* such a facility merely abandoned and not properly shut down could detonate, spreading radioactive material for miles. Known earthquake, flood and landslide country should be avoided for obvious reasons and heavily forested areas should be regarded with great caution. Forest fires in many such locations are a considerable danger even in ordinary times from natural causes. During a crisis, when there is no one to put them out, that danger could be multiplied many times over, particularly when you consider that the woods are likely to be filled with the refugees from the cities—many of whom may be less than expert in handling wilderness campfires.

Nearby military bases or National Guard armories could also pose some significant problems. Even if the troops stationed there did not decide to expropriate the supplies of those living in the vicinity, you might expect the bases to be looted sooner or later and few retreats would be proof against attacks with armored vehicles, flame throwers and grenades.

Whatever your view of the possibility of nuclear war, it seems foolish to me to ignore potential target areas and fallout patterns in selecting a retreat site. If you are going to the considerable trouble and expense of establishing a retreat in the first place, you may as well have one that is secure against as many perils as possible.

These generalized criteria, coupled with your own personal requirements and such other considerations as reasonable climate, factors suitable to agriculture, the availability of some hunting, fishing and trapping will considerably narrow your search for a geographical area in which to locate your retreat, but one major question remains: Do you attempt to go it alone in complete isolation or do you join with others who share your concerns?

The question almost answers itself—at least partially—because regardless of where you choose to locate, there is no retreat site in the continental United States where you could be certain of living in total isolation, completely undetected. Clearly there are places where the odds of discovery would be greatly in your favor, but if you should be stumbled upon by looters, remote from any possible aid, the superior force would almost certainly prevail. Further, if your security were to depend on remaining undiscovered for an extended period of time, the hardships and limitations placed upon you would be enormous. For one thing, raising animals for food would be virtually impossible and even cultivating a garden conveniently near would be a hazard. The emotional strain of keeping constantly quiet and hidden would also be burdensome to most.

For these reasons, and many others that become obvious when you think seriously about the problems of establishing an isolated, single family retreat, one is tempted either to opt for a group retreat—despite their obvious shortcomings—or else remain paralyzed from indecision, doing nothing as time runs out.

Although the problems I observed with existing group retreats invalidated them from practical consideration so far as I was concerned, I remained convinced that only a community of reasonable size with a balance of vital skills would be both workable for the long term and proof against attack by the determined bands of well-organized looters which seem bound to emerge from the crisis period.

The empirical answer to this dilemma, which the theoreticians seem to have missed, is obvious: an already existing, functioning community in which the balance of skills, social interplay and other essential factors have been established pragmatically. A small town.

Not just any small town will do however. It should meet the stringent requirements for any good retreat and offer certain advantages of flexibility as well.

THE SMALL RURAL COMMUNITY

If you place a frog in a pan of boiling water, it will immediately leap out. But start with the water at room temperature, apply heat gradually and the frog will remain in the pan until he is boiled to death.

I am concerned that a substantial number of people who believe that a catastrophe is coming and who see the need for survival preparedness may suffer a similar fate because they are convinced that they will be able to perceive the warning signals and flee to their retreats just in the nick of time. Unfortunately, that sort of thinking makes for victims, not survivors.

There will probably be no warning at all and unless you are living at your retreat when the first blast occurs, the odds are that you will never reach it. As an example, if the collapse develops from economic and political causes, the chances are that its coming will be so gradual that you will wait too long to leave .... I'm not, here, predicting when an economic collapse will occur, but I *am* saying that every-

44

thing necessary to cause such a catastrophe is now in place.

This preamble is meant to point up one of the primary advantages of locating your retreat in a small rural community, as opposed to following one of the more radical cliché alternatives (i.e. isolated wilderness retreats, commercial group retreats, sea or land mobile retreats). You can move there now and live comfortably with whatever conveniences your means allow, for whatever period of grace we may have before the breakdown occurs, and by doing so, you can eliminate the two greatest risks in the survival equation: 1. Estimating or recognizing the time when you should leave for your retreat and 2. the hazardous travel that might be involved in getting there when the crisis actually occurs.

Another advantage of relocating now is that establishing your retreat gives focus to the rest of your plans. It is one thing to know that you will want a generator, for example, quite another to know which generator to buy when you have no idea of how or where it may be used. Similarly, choosing your retreat now will simplify the selection of clothing, storable food, firearms, ammunition and other supplies that you will want to put by. Further, if you are to realize the full advantage of retreating in a small rural community, it is extremely important that you allow enough time before the trouble starts for you to become a part of that community. The last thing you want is to be the stranger—perhaps the expendable stranger—who just blew into town before the crunch began.

From my own experience I can testify that one of the most prudent reasons for moving to a rural retreat now is the development time involved. If you really intend to try having a self-sufficient farm or ranch, you will need as much lead time as you can get before the crisis hits. Even the best small farms will seldom be ideal for your purposes. Most of them rely heavily on electrical power for irrigation and pumping drinking water and many employ electrical cattle fencing. Almost all are dependent on a tractor or other farm machinery for maximum productivity and few farmhouses or outbuildings approach a standard that you or I might recognize as energy efficient. Many small operations have come to employ flood irrigation, a process that leaches nutrients from the soil so rapidly that annual, heavy applications of fertilizer are mandatory.

If you are new to farming or ranching, you should have at least a full year for experimenting with various crops and animals in order to decide what you want to raise before your life depends upon it. You will also need to learn by experience from your own operation just what equipment and supplies you should stockpile. *The First Time Farmer's Guide* and the various other guidebooks are useful, but none of them is a fair substitute for spending four seasons on your own land trying to outwit the invisible bugs that are eating your corn, aiding at the birth of a litter of pigs, sitting up all night with a shotgun across your knees to end the career of a weasel that has killed six of your best laying hens or trying to entice a steer with the brains of an ice cube into the feeding pen through the same hole in the fence he just came out of.

Judging from the mail and calls I receive, a word about the house itself seems in order here. Whether you build or simply remodel, maintain an exterior appearance in keeping with the houses around you—no concrete tepees surrounded by moats, rammed earth underground forts, stainless steel yurts, bulletproof geodesic domes or any of the other configurations that shout "retreat." You do not want your home to attract undue attention, either by its grandeur or its unique appearance.

Selecting A Small Town Retreat

1. SIZE AND COMPOSITION. The community you choose must be small—one to 5,000 population, preferably, and 2,000-3,000 optimally. You are looking for

a community large enough to be proof against any outside attack short of one by an armored division and still small enough to remain cohesive during hard times, with a minuscule disruptive element. Just because a small town has fewer people than a city is no guarantee that it will be nirvana for retreaters. I would consider 20,000 the upper limit even in unusual circumstances because communications and direction become virtually impossible when the population is larger.

Also, the community must be essentially rural—a small industrial town will not do. The economy should be based on small individually owned farms producing a broad variety of crops and livestock. What might be termed "subsistence truck farms" would be ideal. Avoid one-crop areas where vast amounts of grain or some other specialized item is produced but where other food consumed by the population must be imported. Make certain that no substantial number of the residents depend upon government employment, industry or large agribusiness. Imagine what might happen in the small town of Hershey, PA, for example, if the chocolate plant closed.

2. ISOLATION. The community you select should be at least a tank of gasoline removed from any large city and far enough away from even moderately-sized population centers to be truly self-sufficient. All of the vital skills should be present and there should be enough practitioners of them. A quick look at the yellow pages in the local phone book will provide the necessary information on this point.

3. LOCATION. It should be obvious that you will want to avoid areas plagued by natural disasters such as earthquakes, floods, high winds, forest fires and the like. Coastal areas are, similarly, a poor choice because of the possibility of tidal waves. Also to be avoided are all areas of high ambient population. You can be well away from cities and still have too many people around for the best security. Resorts, college towns, tourist areas and similar locales having a large seasonal population upon which the local

economy depends are better avoided even when other criteria are met. Conspicuous food producing locations promise particularly high risks, since they are probably the first places starving mobs escaping the cities would think to run. Military bases, National Guard Armories and nuclear power plants in the vicinity are unacceptable hazards for obvious reasons. Personally, I would also take into account nuclear fallout patterns and I urge you to do so as well, even if you don't presently feel that a nuclear exchange poses a high risk factor. It seems imprudent not to eliminate as many credible perils as possible in an undertaking of this sort.

4. CLIMATE. This is a difficult topic because there is much evidence that our climate is changing, but there are a few points worth considering. From what I have read, the climatic changes trend toward greater cold, so it seems prudent to avoid already severe weather patterns. Further, milder weather will allow you to reduce the amount of clothing and fuel you will need just to stay alive. You will also want to look for a good growing season (160-180 days) and moderate rainfall tending—if toward any extreme—toward the wet. Except in flood-prone areas, too much rain is generally less of a problem than too little. Drought can disrupt all of your survival plans. (Another good reason to lay in plenty of storage food even if you plan to grow your own.)

5. STATE GOVERNMENT. It is important that you give some thought to the government of the state in which you choose your small town. Obviously, it is an advantage to select a state with relatively small government which has no pretensions to national leadership and which provides its officials with no great springboard to national politics. The more services which the state government provides the more taxes will be extracted from you. Smaller state governments also interfere less in your life generally. There are fewer restrictions on what you can do, buy or build and

there are fewer officials to enforce the restrictions on the books.

You should particularly look into the state's gun and hunting laws. There should be no unnecessary red tape when purchasing firearms and ammunition, and concealed weapons permits should be reasonably available to those who qualify for them. It's also helpful if the hunting laws do not proscribe the use of handguns and primitive arms since you will probably want to practice taking game with both after you relocate.

6. PEOPLE. There is an inherent social discipline in small towns. There is no anonymity and, perhaps for that reason, the people tend to have a strong sense of responsibility. Further, unproductive people who are unwilling to work are seldom attracted to farm communities. Farmers are usually disciplined because their work demands it. If you have a cow, she has to be milked twice a day *everyday* at the same hours. Such people are already accustomed to working together for barn raisings, harvest and the like. Also, barter is a way of life: lamb for pork, butter for eggs, hay for grain or labor for a share of the crop. These are the kinds of folk who would band together in a crisis to protect their community from outsiders. They have worked for what is theirs, they take pride in it and they are determined to keep it.

There are, of course, a few sociopaths in every town, I suppose, but in a rural population of two or three thousand, that number is very small indeed—probably no more than the cartridges contained in a single .45 magazine.

Finding the Right Property

When you are outlining your needs to a realtor (discreetly), *don't* tell him you want something remote. The whole point of small town retreating is to obtain the benefits of a *de facto* group retreat without the drawbacks of creating an artificial assembly. If you choose a farm 15 miles away from town down a dead-end road, you might just as well go back to the isolated wilderness cabin concept —in fact, you would probably be better off if you did. When the trouble comes, the greatest value of a small community is that it can become an enclave, excluding danger from without and trading goods, services and social contact within. You must, therefore, be within the probable confines of the enclave if your proximity to others during the crisis is to contribute to your safety and general welfare.

For those of you who are serious about survival relocation there will be dozens of questions in your minds that remain unanswered here. How do you make a living after you move, how do you find a specific property that suits your needs and the like. There *are* viable answers, but space doesn't permit in-depth coverage here. Do not use unanswered questions as excuses for not taking action, however.

Much as I abhor being dogmatic, I see no viable alternative to relocating to a small rural community, if you believe as I do that we are on the verge of a catastrophic social upheaval. Arguments against the position are all ultimately irrelevant if you regard survival as a priority, just as arguments against breathing are irrelevant, no matter how persuasively an expert might insist that polluted air can damage your lungs. There are difficulties, of course, but they must be regarded as necessary adjustments, not reasons for choosing a wholly untenable course of action.

There is simply no tactful way to say this, so I will be blunt: Compromises in the location of your retreat are likely to get you killed. Never mind that you have friends in upstate New York or that you prefer Florida's climate and proximity to beaches or that there's no Junior League chapter for your wife to transfer into. Either you are sufficiently committed to the retreat concept so that you will choose a location with cold-blooded objectivity or you are not. If you are not, you might as well forget the whole idea. Halfway measures will not serve.

LIVING OFF THE LAND

I approach this topic with some misgivings. Nothing in the field seems to generate as much controversy and, frequently, outright hostility as the question of whether living off the land is a viable approach to long-term disaster survival. At the risk of being required to turn in my fire drill, snare wire and obsidian knife, I intend to answer that question forthrightly, in the great tradition of acknowledged experts everywhere: yes and no.

Obviously, the answer is "yes," at some level of technology, because we all draw our sustenance from nature every day. If, however, your idea of living off the land is heading for the nearest woods with nothing more than a backpack and a gleam of confidence in your eye, then I would rate your chances of surviving the sort of catastrophe which this column contemplates as somewhere between zero and none.

Like thumbsucking in children, this notion of escaping a holocaust and subsisting on forage in the wilderness seems to be a phase that all of us must go through when faced with a high probability that the fragile symbiosis of our current urbanized social order may fragment into chaos as a result of runaway inflation or nuclear war.

Before I begin to sound like a temperance league activist leading a roomful of alcoholics in a chorus of "lips that touch liquor shall never touch mine," let me hasten to add that I am no less susceptible to the siren call of the wild than you. I grew up daydreaming over the writings of Nessmuk, Horace Kephart, Townsend Whelen and Brad Angier, and the appeal of cruising real wilderness for a few weeks or even months is certainly not lost on me. Nevertheless, the arguments against the "mountain man" approach to long-term survival are telling—even for experienced woodsmen.

First, if you expect to ensure your safety by hiding, just getting out into the countryside will not do. To have a chance at all you must seek out real wilderness. If you don't, you are almost certain to encounter frightened, desperate mobs of people whose first thought in escaping the cities is the same as yours—head for the nearest patch of woods with whatever can be carried. If there is game in the area, it will quickly be decimated or frightened away. Those who are without supplies, equipment or the skills necessary to provide themselves with food and shelter will undoubtedly try to take what they need by force. Terrified, inexperienced hunters will be shooting at anything that moves; and all around you, first-time woodsmen will be igniting giant fires for warmth and cooking without due regard for safety. The conflagration that will ensue, I leave to your imagination.

If that weren't enough, there is also the matter of logistics. The nomadic aspect of this approach to retreating limits your gear and stores to what you can carry, and you cannot expect resupply. Weight and space considerations will probably confine you to a single firearm and ammunition—probably a centerfire sporting rifle since that option has the potential for providing the most meat for the least expenditure of ammunition. Consider, however, that you would have to take at least eight 125-pound deer to feed a family of two or three for a year exclusively on venison. Further, you might still starve, even with the addition of some plant forage, because such a diet lacks sufficient essential fats.

If small game were also available, you could ill afford to expend cartridges for a mere mouthful of food, and if you did chance a shot, your .30-06 (.308, .270, .30-30) would doubtless turn the critter into pink vapor. Light loads and sub-caliber devices with their attendant ammunition supplies would have to be carefully weighed against the potential of carrying a few more full-power rounds.

Defending yourself from a superior force of attackers

with only a hunting rifle and severely limited ammunition supplies would certainly prove hazardous, particularly at close range in the open where such encounters would probably occur. Finally, stress would exact an enormous toll under these conditions. Virtually every move you made and every decision could mean life or death. Breaking your knife blade or shattering your axe on a hidden pine knot could be a decisive factor in your struggle to stay alive, and the strain of living under such unremitting pressure brings about changes in the human cardio-vascular and endocrine systems that are themselves life threatening.

For those who are caught by the collapse completely unaware, escaping from the population centers into the countryside on shank's mare may be the only alternative, but those of you who see the problems ahead should be armed with a better plan.

A base camp with a permanent shelter located deep enough in true wilderness to stand some chance of escaping detection—however slim—would certainly offer some improvement over "playing Batman in the boondocks." Such an arrangement, however, still fails to tip the balance significantly in favor of the survivalist. You could, of course, stock your cabin in advance and hope to benefit from a wider selection of firearms, more ammunition, reloading supplies, storable foods, books, a wood stove, medical supplies, spares of critical items such as knives and axes. The risks from pilferage and deterioration would not be inconsiderable, however, unless you resorted to fairly elaborate and expensive storage caches. Building a hidden, waterproof, under-ground storage vault, for example, 100 miles by dogsled from the nearest settlement poses some problems.

In addition, there is very little unregulated wilderness any longer where one could build a cabin, take up residence and begin hunting or fishing unmolested. Most of what there is offers such an inhospitable climate and short growing season that cultivating an appreciable amount of food would be out of the question. Keeping domestic animals under those circumstances would probably create a greater number of problems than it would solve.

And then there is the matter of getting to your hide-away. If it is remote enough to do you any good at all, it will probably be several hundred miles from where you live now—and many of those miles should be traversible only by air, pack mule, sled or, possibly, an all-terrain vehicle. If you wait to run until the balloon goes up, the highways will resemble parking lots, airports will be closed or in chaos and you will probably never reach your retreat. If you move there now, you will run the unnecessary risk of being without emergency medical care and lose some of the options that might be available to you if you remained nearer the mainstream of the social order. Forest fires would remain a peril in most locations and, because your entire rationale for security would rest upon your isolation, bartering goods and services would be impossible. Also, you could expect no help from any quarter if you were discovered by a hostile force.

Finally, even in the sort of wilderness we are discussing here, game is now by no means sufficiently plentiful.

Fortunately, neither isolated primitive living nor blundering through the woods with a rucksack exhausts the possibilities of surviving through self-sufficiency. There is at least one viable approach to foraging and living off the land in the aftermath of a disaster.

If wilderness nomadics is one extreme of living off the land, then full-time farming is the other, and it too has its drawbacks. For one thing, making a living solely from working a small farm is so labor intensive and requires so much skill that few people succeed in the attempt. Under survival conditions, of course, you would only need to produce enough to feed your family and, perhaps, a bit more for barter, but even that modest goal involves considerably more knowledge and work than the uninitiated may imagine. Insects, animals, thieves and the weather can all thwart your plans even if you know when, what and where to plant, how to cultivate, rotate and keep your land fertile without the use of commercial fertilizers, and all the rest.

Fortunately, there is a middle ground between these two extremes of seeking long-term subsistence from the land: a thoughtful combination of foraging for wild food and limited small scale agriculture. Although unusual, this approach is practical—as I can personally affirm from almost three years experience with it—and it can save you a great deal of money when you purchase the land for your retreat.

There is often a greater abundance of food more easily available on an abandoned farmstead in good game country than can be found on ten times the acreage in true wilderness. Yet the most expensive farmland is usually well kept and completely cleared to maximize its use for cultivated crops. It offers little in the way of cover for game, and hardy nutritious plants such as dandelions, lamb's quarters, Jerusalem artichokes and thistles, which flourish without care in most parts of the country, have been uprooted and burned as unwanted weeds. That is a logical approach for the full-time farmer whose eye is on developing cash crops for market, but for the survivalist who is concerned with producing the surest source of nutrition for his family with the least amount of work, it is a serious mistake.

An optimal retreat site for the survivalist forager might be a poorly maintained or abandoned small farm, a portion of which had once been cultivated but which had never been entirely cleared of trees. You might even want to add additional brush piles for small game cover, and, if a suitable one does not already exist, you should consider digging a pond. Nothing else will enhance the food producing potential of your land as much, even if you don't bother —as you should—to stock it with fish. Turtles and frogs will appear as if by magic, deer and other large game may be attracted if the terrain and certain other conditions are right, flocks of migratory birds will probably come in if you are near a flyway and a variety of edible small game such as muskrat will undoubtedly take up residence there. The pond doesn't need to be more than a few feet deep unless you will require a great deal of irrigation water from it, but the surface area should be as large as you can reasonably make it, for maximum effect. A two-acre pond on an eight to ten-acre parcel is none too large. Surrounded by a start of such nourishing edibles as wild rice, cattails, berry bushes and the like, then stocked with trout, catfish or bass and bluegills—depending on location and climate—such a pond alone could provide substantially all of the food necessary for a small family.

Before you decide on a location for your pond or clear a square-inch of land, however, you should get a good book on plant identification such as Brad Angier's *Feasting Free on Wild Edibles* and a deck of the excellent full-color cards for your region with a photograph of each native wild plant on one side and data concerning its value on the other, offered by Survival, Inc. (17019 Kingsview, Carson, CA 90746, $6.45 postpaid). Then walk your entire property with a notebook, listing and marking the location of everything that grows there. You may want to remove and destroy all poisonous or otherwise harmful plants and, perhaps, introduce some edibles that flourish in your neighborhood but are not well represented on your land.

A few fruit and nut trees should also be considered, not only for their relatively carefree harvest but also to attract more game. Prudence dictates having a garden, despite the work involved, but it need not be large. A plot 50x70 feet, properly handled, will provide all the produce a family of four can use. Twice that area would yield an abundance for both storage (canning, dehydration, etc.) and barter.

Most survivalists forget about growing grains. You shouldn't, but neither should you consider the kind of labor intensive cultivation and machine harvest used by agribusiness. The five bushels of grain consumed by the average American family can easily be grown on 1/6 of an acre—a plot 75x100 feet—and harvested by hand. If you have farm animals, you may want a bit more to increase egg production or improve the quality of your beef—and nothing else will attract wild game birds as quickly as a few stands of grain sown along your fence lines.

Harvesting your cultivated crops and slaughtering your farm animals for the table, if something of a chore, requires little instruction, and foraging for wild plant edibles takes little more effort than a casual stroll; no more equipment than a garden trowel or a stout, oversized sheath knife and a deck of plant identification cards in your pocket. The kind of hunting you will encounter under the circumstances outlined here, however, is apt to call for some specialized knowledge, different tools and an overall approach to which you may be unaccustomed. Foraging is *not* sport hunting and, under survival conditions, the consequences of an empty game bag are considerably more serious than merely being the butt of some good natured, if crude, humor at day's end.

If you really expect to succeed living off the land, you will almost never "go hunting." It is too time consuming for the amount of food produced, yet you should always be prepared to take a mixed bag, as it is presented, whenever you are outdoors at your retreat. Small farms develop a certain rhythm which the animals perceive and they expose themselves much more frequently when you are performing routine chores than when you are "hunting." The problem is, when you set out for the day's work, you never know what you may have the opportunity to garner: a few giant bullfrogs or a couple of snapping turtles sunning themselves on a log as you pass the pond, quail or pheasant flushing ahead of you as you enter the pasture or, perhaps, a deer helping himself to the salt lick you so carefully provided near the orchard. You may also encounter a variety of pests that need eliminating, from rats in the feed bin to coyotes stalking your new lambs. Obviously, you will need to be armed routinely, but with what? Your Sunday-best scoped centerfire rifle will seldom be needed for such service and after a few months aboard the tractor or parting brush and being dropped in thickets, it might pass as a relic of the Boer War. Besides, such a rifle would not offer sufficient versatility and would be too cumbersome for daily carry. A shotgun? Better, perhaps, but certainly not ideal for frogs and turtles or long shots at varmints.

The wear and rough handling that long guns are almost certain to receive under these circumstances seems to call for simple, reliable utility arms. In particular, I have found the Savage 24 series combination guns virtually indispensable in such service. The short, hardy 24C takedown Camper's Model with a .22 rimfire rifle barrel superposed over a 20 gauge smoothbore is especially suitable. The hollow butt holds extra ammunition and the rifle is far more accurate than either the gun's appearance or its modest price would indicate. A switch that falls naturally under your thumb on the hammer when you cock the piece provides an instant choice of either shotgun or rifle. Coupled with a short, big-bore handgun, you are prepared to meet almost any foraging challenge your farmstead may offer. Another useful pair of combinations are the Savage 24V, .357 Magnum over 20 gauge, together with a compact, high quality, accurate rimfire pistol such as the Walther PP or Smith & Wesson Kit Gun, and Marlin's diminutive new lever-action .357 Magnum carbine carried with a choked Thompson/Center Contender chambered for .410 three-inch shells (actually, a .45 Colt barrel with detachable choke and the chamber deepened).

Most of the animal life you can bring to bag at a farm retreat will be potentially edible and, probably, highly nutritious, but you may never learn how to make it palatable without some expert guidance. For this reason, include some of the better wild food cookbooks in your survival library and make sure that they cover not only recipes for the customary game animals, but instructions on preparing the more common small farm denizens and unusual plants as well. I especially recommend Euell Gibbons' "Stalking" series (*Stalking the Wild Asparagus, Stalking the Blue-Eyed Scallop,* etc.) and Brad Angier's *Home Book of Cooking Venison and Other Natural Meats.*

Almost anyone *can* gain the necessary skill to provide a full larder of wild food by taking advantage of the great variety of edibles freely available on uncultivated land in rural areas. If you do, you may increase your health by replacing the stale, over-processed, chemically laden food in your diet, gain peace of mind from knowing that you *can* live off the land in an emergency and derive satisfaction from self-reliance that no amount of plucking plastic wrapped packages from the supermarket shelf could ever bring. And when the time comes that the supermarket shelf is no longer there—you could save your life.

QUESTIONS & ANSWERS

Q: Sirs:

I wagered 50¢ with my husband that you would not print my letter because:

a) it was written by a woman and

b) it criticized one of your sacred bulls, namely, Mel Tappan. I note that he has not dealt with any of the questions I raised, namely and to wit:

1. How many groups does he expect to adopt his plan?

2. How can he guarantee safe water to them?

3. Where will be found enough available ten acre spots that meet his criteria—"wooded property with a good water supply, a reasonable climate with good growing season and an abundance of both large and small game"— all 300 or more miles from an urban center?

4. How long would the game continue to be abundant?

5. How many people can a ten acre plot support? For how long?

6. How many of these people know how to live on a subsistence farm?

7. How will they cope with snakebite, gangrene, and appendicitis?

8. Does he intend to take in enough ammunition to last indefinitely?

9. What experience has Mr. Tappan had on a year round basis of totally self-sufficient living? Mrs. C.A.B., CA

A: What I have been trying to get across in these columns is this: Because of government debasement of the currency and other reasons, we are obviously in for a serious upheaval—at least in this country and perhaps in the world—rather soon. Since we have very little chance, collectively, of stopping this juggernaut toward bankruptcy in the time we have left, it makes sense to me that we expend some time, money, and effort in preparations to minimize the effects of such a disaster on an individual basis. I am suggesting that each of us to whom this concept seems reasonable take whatever steps appear prudent to become less dependent on the uninterrupted functioning of our highly complex, interdependent social order and to become more nearly self-sufficient with respect to basic life supports.

In that context, let me address the questions briefly and in order.

1. I am writing for individuals, not "groups," and if even a handful are better prepared than they would have been otherwise, I consider my efforts worthwhile. To the extent that some are prepared to care for themselves in a crisis, there will be that much less demand on whatever emergency systems remain. Judging from the number of people who consult me professionally and the response to my book and to this column, the percentage could be significant.

2. Would you expect me to change your tire and

guarantee you against future automotive troubles if I warned you of a puncture?

3. There probably isn't enough suitable land for everyone in this country to have an optimal retreat here, but then, if everyone were sufficiently aware of and concerned with the problem, there would be no need for retreats. Practically speaking, there are more than enough good sites to meet the needs of those who have the wisdom to seek them.

4. Not very long, but I would expect that anyone surviving the crisis period would have the wit to trap animals for breeding and plant a garden before his stored food was exhausted.

5. Ten acres can support four to ten people indefinitely, depending upon the quality of the soil, available water, management skill and other factors.

6. I assume that anyone serious enough to seek a retreat will also seek the knowledge necessary to make it work. I have dozens of clients who have learned rather quickly. There is no magic about learning to provide for your own needs, otherwise the human race would have died out in the Stone Age. The information, skills and techniques are available to anyone who is sufficiently motivated.

7. A future article in this series will deal with the medical problems of self-sufficient living.

8. Who knows what is "enough" ammunition? A good hunter can provide a year's meat with a handful of cartridges. If you are drawn into a sustained fire fight with a band of looters, however, a thousand rounds might be expended on a single occasion. It seems reasonable that one would be in a better position trying to store "enough" than making no attempt at all to be prepared.

9. The skills attendant to self-sufficient living have been a lifelong interest and subject of study for me. From time to time, circumstances have provided more than my share of occasions to test the survival skills I've developed and I have been consulting, writing and conducting seminars in

the field for a number of years. My wife and I presently live on a self-sufficient ranch.

Q: My wife and I have moved to the country as a direct result of reading your column and your book, *Survival Guns*. We are just beginning to raise some livestock and find it pretty heavy going with no experience at all between us. Can you offer any general advice and would you recommend some good books on animal treatment? J.E., MT

A: The best brief advice I can give you on raising farm animals is "go slowly." Try only a few head of livestock at a time and experiment with a broad variety. All animals are a lot of trouble to care for, so you'd better find the kind you can learn to love before you take them on in quantity.

One classic reference book is the *Merck Veterinary Manual*. It is excellent but quite condensed and rather technical. Two very thorough and readable books by practicing veterinarians are: *Animal Husbandry* by Guy Lockwood, D.V.M. and *A Veterinary Guide For Animal Owners* by C.E. Spaulding, D.V.M. Also helpful are *Raising Small Livestock* by Jerome D. Belanger and Carla Emery's compendium on country living, *Old Fashioned Recipe Book*.

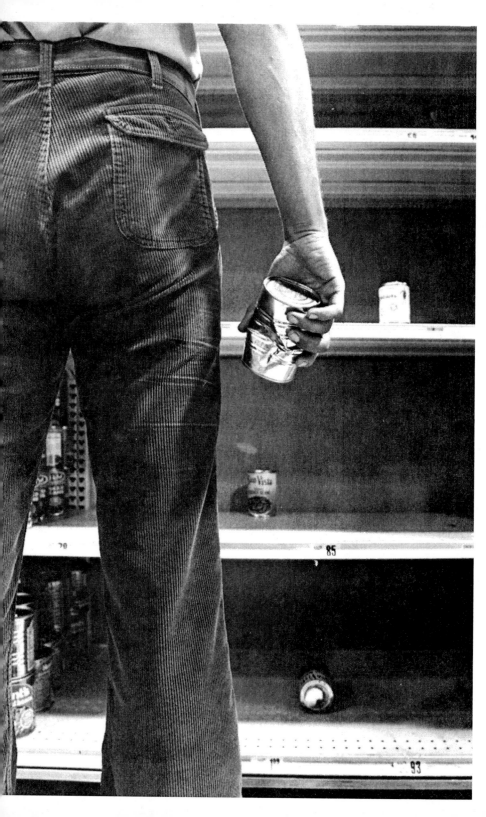

4.

FOOD STORAGE

I invite you to try an experiment. Take a pad of paper and jot down all of the food you have in your house. If you are honest about the quantities you consume and if you are close to the national average, you will probably have something slightly less than a week's supply on hand. Consider how well you might fare if your town were paralyzed by a snowstorm as Buffalo was this winter, or if an earthquake, flood or windstorm struck. For that matter, consider the results of even more personal disasters such as a severe accident or the loss of your job. If you find this awareness of your vulnerability sobering, you will not be cheered by the fact that the food supply of an average U.S. city is only eight days or that the total amount of food in the world has dropped from a tenuous 180 days' ration to less than 84. Couple these emergency conditions with the long-term outlook alluded to earlier and you should have enough information to view your own circumstances in an atmosphere of reasonable concern.

Although there may be nothing we can do to alleviate

these problems or even to prevent them from becoming increasingly acute, we can—as individuals—take steps to protect ourselves and our families from the devastation which the contingencies I have outlined are almost certain to provoke.

The obvious answer to the possibility of future food shortages is to buy and store a supply now while it is available and affordable, and to make provision for supplementing or renewing that supply by growing your own, hunting and bartering with hard goods later. Implementing a sound food storage program is easier than it may sound and it is well within the means of the average American family. There are some pitfalls, of course, but the information contained here should allow you to tailor a storage program suited to your needs and to avoid the more costly errors.

The amount of food you choose to store should be based upon your own assessment of how severe and long lasting the shortages may be, but even an inadequate supply is better than nothing because it will buy you time. For most people, a one year program is a barely comfortable minimum and two years' is better. If you can afford it, even a five year supply is not unreasonable since you can almost certainly trade any excess for other items which you may need. And you can, of course, simply eat your food if your concerns later prove to be unfounded.

Buying one of the numerous, preselected, so-called "one year" or "survival" food packages produced by various suppliers is certainly the easiest approach to food storage and one which many dealers will recommend or even push. In most cases these package deals are inappropriate and in many, they are dangerously inadequate. For one thing, they often provide no more than 900 or 1100 calories per day—hardly an adequate ration for an active adult, particularly under conditions of stress. For another, few companies prepare all of their foods equally well, and you may be better off choosing the items you want from several different packagers. Finally, it makes no more sense to purchase a standardized or prepackaged food storage program than it does to buy your weekly bag of groceries selected and bagged by a supermarket clerk, without regard to your personal preferences. If at all possible, you should sample a variety of storable foods before you make large purchases. One of the most convenient ways I have found to introduce clients to the better quality foods prepared for long-term storage is to have them order the sampler put up by Survival, Inc. (Survival, Inc., 17019 Kingsview, Carson, CA 90746, $47.50 postpaid). It contains generous portions of twelve storage foods, both air-dried and freeze-dried, and from it you can easily build a program which will suit your taste. Take warning, however. Some of the items contained in this sampler—such as the Mountain House sausage—are so tasty that you will want to include them in your regular diet.

Ideally, you should counsel with someone knowledgeable in food storage whom you can trust, but you can probably avoid any serious blunders by following a basic plan which I have recommended to many of my clients. First acquire an *honest* three months' supply of "wet pack" or ordinary canned goods and other supermarket foods which you consume on a regular basis. Try to provide about 2000+ calories a day and a good balance of foods you really like. A mixed case of chili and potato soup is *not* a true month's supply, even though it may look like a lot in terms of what you are used to keeping on your shelves. If you are unsure about quantities, try writing down the type and amount of every food item your family consumes for a week and then multiply by 13. It is a good idea to date stamp your canned goods and rotate them so that your supply will always be as fresh as possible in an emergency. Most canned products retain substantially all of their nutritive value for at least a year and they remain safe to eat—assuming no bulged cans or other evidence of spoilage—for as long as three years.

Both the food value and the shelf life can be extended if you turn each can upside down once a month. These supplies should see you through such short-term emergencies as earthquakes, floods, storms, strikes, temporary shortages, power outages and the like, but they will not last long enough to provide the basis for a major storage program.

Next I recommend a highly portable three months supply which requires little, if any, energy for preparation. This portion of your program should be considered part of your emergency "flight kit" and it should be stored with those essential items which you would take with you if a flood, fire or other emergency should require evacuating your home or retreat. Here, freeze-dried foods are optimal, since they require no cooking, only boiling water to prepare, and some items can even be eaten dry just as they come from the package. Ideally, complete meals or groups of meals should be packaged together in easy to handle containers. No better quality in this type of food or packaging is available than that sold by Oregon Freeze Dry Foods, Inc. under the brand name, "Mountain House." An especially handy 8-day unit of Mountain House complete meals is marketed as the "Emergency 6-pack." It contains six #10 vacuum packed cans—two of breakfasts, two of lunches and two of dinners—all sealed in an under-arm sized corrugated box bearing a detailed contents label. Shelf life of the unopened cans is about 15 years and the price, postpaid from Survival, Inc. is $56.

The balance of your program might be comprised of vacuum packed freeze-dried and air-dried fruits and vegetables, freeze-dried meats and complete main courses such as beef stew, chicken and rice, or whatever else suits your taste and your budget. Only a few of the air-dry processors are using the latest vacuum methods today, but that—and not the older "probe" technique—is what you want, and you will have to depend on a reliable dealer to be certain that you get it. There are simply too many air-dry labels to list them and the methods employed by their packagers here.

Only you can determine how much food you want to store and what price you are willing to pay now for future self-sufficiency, but these are not the only variables to be considered before you buy. In addition to overall cost, you should know just how many calories you are getting for your dollar, the quality and nutritional balance of each item you put by, the kind of processing and the type of packaging employed, the anticipated shelf life, the preparation required and the palatability. There are scores of brands and qualities presently being offered by storable food sales organizations. Some of them are superb, others are barely adequate and quite a few are simply unsatisfactory. Price, incidentally, is not always a reliable guide to quality in this field. I know of at least one very expensive so-called "year's supply" program, widely touted by a self-styled "expert," which consists largely of mashed potatoes, peas and grains. The calories are abundant, but the nutritional balance leaves a good deal to be desired.

Except for grains, most of the items I recommend for long-term storage are dehydrated—by one technique or another—and vacuum packed. Such processing offers both good taste and substantial shelf life—often 15 years or longer. Within this category, however, there are still some notable differences which you should take into account.

One of the most important is the quality of fresh food that the packer begins with, and here again, price is not necessarily a reliable indicator. Unfortunately, unless you have access to the packer's warehouse or are willing to spend the time and money required to have some comparative tests conducted, you will have to rely on professional advice, the reputation of the packer, or the word of the merchant from whom you buy.

Although there are many companies who do not pack the very best grade of food available, almost none of the better known brands uses the worst. One might be tempted to take cold comfort from that statement, were it not for the fact that the methods of processing and packaging have at least as much to do with the overall quality of the storable product as the grade of food that goes into it.

The two most common techniques for dehydrating food are air drying and freeze drying. Each has certain advantages and disadvantages which should be evaluated in terms of your own requirements and preferences. In air drying, the raw food is exposed to a controlled flow of warm, dry air until substantially all of the moisture has been removed. Preservatives are often added and then the product is sealed, usually in enameled cans. Except for fruits, you must both cook and return the moisture to air-dried foods—usually by boiling for about 20 minutes—since they were raw before being dehydrated.

The freeze drying process, on the other hand, customarily begins with full or partial cooking, then the item is flash frozen and a vacuum is drawn while heat is applied so that the moisture goes directly from ice to vapor without passing through the liquid stage. Normally, only the addition of boiling water is necessary for a table-ready hot meal. Freeze-dried products are generally more expensive than air-dried and less compact (except when they are also compressed—a still costlier technique).They require less time, trouble and energy to prepare, however, and some items—such as meats and a few fruits (pineapples, blueberries, etc.) are *only* available freeze-dried. Completely prepared main courses such as shrimp creole, chicken stew, tuna or chicken salad may also be had freeze-dried. Air-dried units usually substitute TVP (textured vegetable protein) for meat. Since there is considerable debate regarding the nutritional value of TVP and treating the controversy fairly would require more space than I have here, I will merely note that the flavored versions normally contain more preservatives and salt than I care to ingest, but the unflavored granules may have a place as ground meat extenders and soup thickeners. Given equal packaging, air-dried and freeze-dried products have about the same shelf life—so long as they remain sealed. But once the cans are opened, the air-dried will keep longer—from six months to three years, compared to one to six months for freeze-dried. In either case, incidentally, the plastic lids which should be supplied with each No. 10 storage can ought to be tightly replaced after each use.

Heated arguments tend to arise when the various packing methods are discussed by their adherents, so I will simply describe the three most common ones here and let you be the judge of which best suits your needs. The technique employed does not usually influence the retail price of the product.

VACUUM BOX: The filled can of dehydrated food, with the lid loosely in place, is enclosed in an airtight box. A vacuum is drawn to 29½ inches of mercury and held until the air is exhausted as nearly as possible from the product. The chamber is then flooded with an inert gas (usually nitrogen) and the can is sealed before being removed from the controlled atmosphere.

DRY CANNING: Here, the can is simply filled and sealed. No attempt is made either to remove ambient oxygen or to introduce an inert atmosphere.

PROBE METHOD: Falling in between the other two techniques, the probe method attempts partially to evacuate oxygen and to provide a nitrogen atmosphere by the expedient of thrusting a flexible tube into the filled can and pumping the heavier-than-air gas through it until the operator decides that enough air has been replaced. The can is then sealed by ordinary means.

Personally, I prefer the vacuum box method, even though some argue that the amount of residual oxygen left in the cans does not cause the food in them to oxidize or age any faster. The *Mountain House* freeze-dried brand by Oregon Freeze Dry Foods, Inc. and the *Country Cupboard* air-dried private label by Ready Reserve both use the vacuum box technique, and samples of each may be obtained by writing to Survival, Inc., 17019 Kingsview, Carson, CA 90746.

Many people find—and I am among them—that air-dried fruits and vegetables suit their palates at least as well as freeze-dried. Since they are cheaper and store just as well, I prefer them in my own storage program, along with air-dried non-instant powdered milk (about 100 lbs. per person per year). I buy freeze-dried meats, strawberries and prepared main courses, however. Whichever type of vegetables you select, you will find their flavor greatly enhanced by placing a spoonful of sugar or honey in the water with which you reconstitute each serving for two.

Wheat or flour, sugar or honey, salt and salad oil—all vacuum packed—will round out a basic storage unit. Butter powder, shortening powder, and peanut butter powder—all to be mixed with salad oil—will add greatly to the variety of your menus. Yeast and baking powder both have limited storage lives, so you will probably want to include a powdered culture for starting a sourdough mix— and fellow yogurt lovers will doubtless store their favorite brands of starter for use with powdered milk.

Most people would also do well to include vitamin supplements—at least a potent multivitamin (gerontological formulas are especially good)—and a supply of vitamin C, since it does not preserve well in foods. Consult your physician or a nutritionist if you are in doubt about what you need.

Whatever you do, don't skimp on seasonings. These are among the cheapest, easiest to store and most useful items that you can include in your survival preparations. Pepper, chili powder, allspice, curry powder, basil, thyme, oregano, cinnamon, paprika—along with salt and whatever else suits your taste—can make an astonishing difference if you are ever forced to live on emergency rations. You may have to supplement your stores with unfamiliar game or items of unknown origin, and familiar seasonings can help you accommodate to these strange rations. Curry and chili powders, after all, were originally designed to mask bad meats and poor ingredients.

The food storage program outlined above is very nearly ideal for the average family. The air-dried and freeze-dried items suggested are at least as palatable as most of the frozen and canned goods served daily in many homes and they are considerably better than most convenience foods. Dehydrated products are compact and easy to store. There is virtually no waste and they will remain safely edible almost indefinitely when packaged by the most efficient modern techniques. Finally, a year's supply of even the best quality dried foods prepared for long-term storage costs only 10-15 percent more than you would spend at the supermarket during a year—and it appears almost certain that inflation over the next 12 months will narrow that margin to the vanishing point.

Despite these advantages, some of you will find it useful to consider other approaches to solving the problem of becoming food self-sufficient. For example, if you want to put by more than a one year's supply and can't afford it or, for that matter, if you prefer to start your program with the smallest possible cash outlay, then storing the "basic four" may be a workable alternative for you.

Three hundred pounds of hard red winter wheat, 100 pounds of powdered milk, 100 pounds of honey and eight pounds of salt will sustain a single individual for a year and provide acceptable basic nutrition and about 2000 calories per day. The wheat should be well cleaned but uncracked (to preserve the germ) with low moisture and at least a 12 percent protein content (15 percent is better). The milk should be of the non-fat, non-instant variety. All of these items can be had vacuum packed in an inert nitrogen atmosphere for $300 to $400, depending upon the quality you get and where you buy. The milk should definitely be commercially packaged for storage but you may try putting up the wheat yourself if you must cut corners. New five-gallon enameled steel cans work well. You will need nine of them for each 300 pounds of wheat and they are available from Survival, Inc.

Try placing a fist-sized piece of dry ice in the bottom of each can before filling it with wheat, and then put the lid loosely in place. The evaporating dry ice (CO_2) will at least partially displace the air in the can since it is heavier, and when the lid stops "burping," you can seal it tightly.

The two chief problems encountered in storing wheat for long periods of time are moisture (encourages rot and mold) and air (necessary for insect growth). The dry ice technique will help to exclude both, but it is not as certain as commercial vacuum packaging.

Obviously, such a diet offers little variety, it is marginal in both fat and vitamin C content, but it is viable if you can do no better. It is at its best as an adjunct to a good selection of freeze-dried and air-dried foods and it can be improved greatly by adding vitamin supplements, sprouting and obtaining an outside source of fats. Even a modest amount of fishing, hunting and foraging for edible roots and plants will greatly increase its value. If you decide to try this approach, don't fail to include a hand wheat grinder. A small book called *Passport To Survival* by Esther Dickey contains a variety of ideas on preparing balanced meals using nothing else but these four basic foods.

Another way of saving money on your supplies is to buy fresh food in quantity and process it yourself. Freeze drying is beyond the realm of "do-it-yourself," of course, but air drying is fairly simple. You can buy or build a modest home dehydrator quite reasonably, and the product you can make is at least as good as anything you can buy—assuming that you begin with high quality produce. Air-dried meats become jerky, however, unlike the freeze-dried variety which closely resemble fresh cuts when rehydrated.

The only other serious drawback to this approach is that

you cannot package your home-dehydrated foods as well as the better commercial processors can and, consequently, they will not last as long. I would want to rotate home-dried foods every two or three years at least. Still, it is worth learning to preserve your own foods by drying as well as canning, smoking and other methods since your stored supplies will sooner or later become exhausted and you will need to replace them. The best book I have found describing all of these techniques in detail is *Putting Food By*: Hertzberg, Vaughan, and Greene.

While we are on the subject of learning to replace and supplement the foods in your storage program by your own efforts, I should note that books on hunting, trapping, foraging for wild edibles, and the like are musts for your survival kit unless you are already a practiced expert in all of these fields. And don't overlook books on sprouting, gardening and cooking game and wild plants. I have found the deck of plant identification cards sold by Survival, Inc. particularly useful and I especially recommend Brad Angier's book, *Home Book of Venison and Other Natural Meats*, if you want to know how to prepare almost any animal that you can bring to ground. Euell Gibbon's books on foraging are classics.

To round out your plans for renewing your food resources you will, of course, need to include an ample quantity of garden seeds and beans for both planting and sprouting. Do not select hybrids, however, because many of them require commercial, artificial fertilizers and most do not produce stable seeds for future crops.

One of the wisest purchases you can make for storage is a nitrogen-packed can of assorted non-hybrid garden seeds. This unique item is somewhat more expensive than the seeds you will find regularly available in stores, but the long shelf life and proven high level of germination are worth the added cost for survival use. Two or three cans should be enough—even allowing for a bad crop or two as a result of poor weather or a novice sodbuster.

Although not properly a food, some consideration of a reliable water supply seems appropriate here since without it, no food storage program is viable. Storing water is by no means a complete answer because of the great and continuing need which the body has for it and the amount of space required to keep even a modest supply on hand, but some water should be stored for short-term emergencies in every home, even if you have a well of your own or a stream. Pumps do break down and streams, lakes and even springs can become polluted.

In California, the average person uses about 175 gallons of water per day, and I suspect that the national average is fairly close to that figure. A substantial portion of that amount is used in washing clothes, flushing toilets (5 to 7 gallons with each pull of the chain) and bathing, but about 2 gallons per capita is consumed directly or employed in the preparation of food. Although you could live on less for short periods in a cold or temperate climate if you were inactive, one gallon per person per day is the minimum amount you should consider storing for drinking and preparing food in an emergency.

If you are fortunate enough to have a swimming pool, your storage problem is solved—assuming that you have a small water purifier and that you don't have to leave your pool site. Bizarre as it may sound, a waterbed is another good possibility, particularly if your space is limited. You can either use it as a bed or stand it on its side in a frame made for the purpose and it will require very little floor space. King-size models usually hold from 270 to 300 gallons. If you have the room, empty plastic chlorine bleach bottles are perhaps the simplest and most economical answer. They are cheap, easy to handle even when full and the few remaining drops of bleach which collect in them help to preserve the contents. Whatever you use, avoid any container that ever held petroleum based products, poisons or caustic chemicals.

If you are sure of your water supply when you bottle it,

you need take no special precautions for storage except to make certain that your containers are scrupulously clean and that the closure is air tight. I always add eight drops of 5.25 percent chlorine bleach per gallon as insurance, however. Water from questionable sources can be treated with twice as much bleach and allowed to stand for a half hour. If you can still smell and taste the chlorine at the end of that time, you can be reasonably certain that the water is safe. Tincture of iodine crystals or boiling can also be used, but I prefer the silver-ion and charcoal purifiers such as the thermos-sized 1500 gallon water purifier from Survival, Inc. ($37.50). These will reliably kill bacteria from *E. coli* to *Pseudomonas aeruginosa* and also remove both solids and odors.

Sources for products mentioned in this chapter:
Catalogs available

Survival, Inc., 17019 Kingsview, Carson, CA 90746
$2.00

The Larder, 11106 Magnolia Blvd., N. Hollywood, CA 91601
$2.00

Arrowhead Mills, Inc., Box 866-F, Hereford, TX 79045
no charge

5.

WEAPONS

SURVIVAL BATTERY

If someone asked you to choose the best tool for building a house, how would you reply? Obviously, the question itself indicates a lack of understanding about the complexity of the task. And for this same reason many people feel that selecting arms for long-term survival is a simple matter—particularly if they are knowledgeable gun buffs who already possess a rack full of favorites for hunting and, perhaps, a piece or two for home defense. The same chaps who bay at the moon when a new varmint caliber is announced, agonize for years over the choice of the "ideal" antelope rifle or spend several hundred dollars having a target gun tuned to shrink the group size by ¼ inch will often become positively Spartan when the talk turns to survival. Usually, they will fix you with a glazed eye, drop their voices to a conspiratorial whisper and confide that the "perfect" survival arm is: A) a .22 rimfire, B) a black powder musket or C) a bow and a quiver full of arrows.

This sort of Daniel Boone romanticism would be considerably more amusing if the subject were less critical, but the truth is that staying alive in the aftermath of the kinds of disasters which we have examined in previous columns is not apt to be either easy *or* romantic, and choosing the optimal survival battery for your particular circumstances may be the most important single aspect of your survival planning. Aside from shelter, your two most pressing concerns are likely to be 1) personal defense during a period of unrestrained, mass violence and 2) providing a continuing source of food for yourself and those you care for. Only proper arms and your ability to use them effectively offer a reasonable solution to that premise.

The culprit in most stereotyped thinking about survival is the belief that survival situations *ought to* involve a great deal of improvising. Almost certainly there will be unanticipated circumstances which will force you to improvise, but good planning can confine these to non-critical areas which may involve your comfort but not your safety. If you run out of matches, you can make a fire by at least a dozen other means, given time; but if you are attacked by a band of looters or set upon by feral dogs and you are inadequately armed, it could cost you your life.

There is no moral virtue in being Spartan when you are selecting equipment on which you may have to rely for food and protection over an extended period of time. If you plan a fixed retreat and can possibly afford the cost, it is simply unintelligent not to provide yourself with the very best available—and in some depth. The fact that some people might be able to muddle through with nothing but a .22, a .30-06 and a 12-gauge shotgun does not mean that such arms are enough, any more than driving cross country on a set of bald tires can be regarded as a sound practice even though it may have been done before. No other purchase which you might make in preparation for your survival—with the possible exception of your retreat itself—is likely to have as much to do with whether you stay alive as your survival battery. Unless you are willing to settle for minimum survival odds, do not skimp on your selection of firearms.

As you begin to consider just how extensive your personal survival battery should be, remember that if a social breakdown comes, you may be faced with living under primitive conditions for a year, a decade or even the rest of your life, and your basic life support problems will almost certainly be complicated by encounters with desperate, dangerous mobs of people who have made no crisis preparations of their own and who are anxious to avail themselves of yours by force. Instead of compromise or improvisation, such circumstances call for the most specialized and efficient arms available. Foraging for small game with an assault rifle makes little more sense than trying to stave off a determined attack on your retreat with a bolt-action sporter. Consequently, I am going to suggest that your survival battery include two separate categories of guns: defense and working and that neither should be expected to do double duty.

Working Guns

What I call "working guns" would include arms suitable for both large and small game hunting, predator and pest control—and, if your situation warrants, protection from dangerous animals. Although their levels of power and action types may differ, depending upon your require-ments and preferences, these are nothing more than the sporting guns with which we are all familiar and your selections will doubtless require little comment from me. You should, of course, buy quality and take into account both the terrain and the type of game to be found in your retreat area. Further, I think it's a good idea to stay with the most popular calibers, even if you feel that a wildcat or one of the more exotic production items would be slightly more efficient for your intended purpose. Although you may plan to reload extensively—as you certainly should—you will probably want to lay in a substantial supply of factory ammo because it has a better shelf life than components and it will be more valuable as an item of trade if you find that you have more than you need. Such cartridges as the .308, the .30-06 and rimfire .22s might be worth more than their weight in gold for barter, but you could look for a long time before you found anyone willing to part with a cow in return for a box of .296 Belch Fire Magnums.

All of your scoped rifles should also have a good set of iron sights, and quick detachable mounts are worth considering despite their higher cost. Ease of repair—*by you*—should also be one of your prime criteria and each gun in your battery ought to have its own separately packaged kit of spare parts, worked out carefully in consultation with a good gunsmith and purchased when you buy the gun. Some people prefer to have duplicates of everything, but that approach is so costly that it often precludes your having enough different types and calibers to meet your needs efficiently. A duplicate firearm is a rather expensive spare parts bin and it really does not solve the problem. Parts that tend to break, such as firing pins, tend to break more than once, and two broken firing pins simply mean a pair of guns that don't function.

Except in very unusual circumstances, accurate, reliable centerfire rifles in the .270, .308 or .30-06 power range will be the most essential items in your working battery. They will put more meat on the table per ounce of ammunition expended than any other gun and they will serve—with proper ammunition—for a wide range of uses from pest control to protection from large animals. There are better choices for either extreme, of course, and if you need them, by all means include them in your plans.

A shotgun is more prodigal in terms of the ammunition-to-food ratio, but there are times when nothing else can be relied upon to fill the pot, and at least one good 12-gauge, open-choked scattergun should figure in your plans. Further, smoothbores offer an economical means of using "scrounged" ammunition. With a set of Shell Shrinkers in appropriate calibers and gauges (Harry Owen, Sport Specialties, P.O. Box 5337, Hacienda Heights, CA 91745), you can fire 20, 28 and .410 shotshells as well as a wide variety of popular pistol and rifle cartridges with useful accuracy from almost any 12-gauge shotgun.

A handgun is perhaps less than essential in your working battery but it can be an efficient means of finishing wounded game without excessive meat spoilage and it is, in my opinion, more practical than game rifle sub-loads for taking rabbits, grouse and the like when you are hunting larger animals. If you choose a rimfire for this purpose, several of the pocket autopistols, such as the Walther PPK, offer all the accuracy you can use and they are convenient to carry. Among the centerfires, revolvers make better working guns, not only because they preserve their brass for reloading, but also because you can have several types of loads quickly available—from shot to mild wadcutters to full power—by progressive loading of the chambers.

Defense

Some writers and consultants in the field of disaster survival believe that violence either will not be a significant factor in the aftermath of a social collapse or else that it will be confined to the inner cities of large metropolitan areas. They recommend that your survival preparations be limited to gold and silver coins, storable foods, water purifiers, a portable radio and, possibly, a gun for hunting. I wish I could agree with that point of view, because then I could save both this magazine and myself from the untoward level of criticism which seems to follow inexorably from any forthright discussion of effective, armed personal defense.

Since I cannot in good conscience avoid the topic and I haven't the space to deal with it circumspectly, I will be blunt. Ours is a social order in which disturbances no more serious than a citywide power failure or a "peaceful" "student" demonstration frequently erupt into riots of such proportions that the National Guard is required to quell them. What we might expect in the wake of a monetary collapse, nuclear attack or accident, famine or terrorist inspired revolution, I leave to your imagination.

You may escape the more concentrated chaos of the cities if you have a sufficiently remote retreat and the good sense to occupy it before the bell rings, but no haven on earth can be regarded as completely safe from discovery and, if your timing is off, you may even have to fight to get there.

Now I realize that most readers of this magazine probably have some sort of firearm around the house, but the level of security called for in this context requires more than a casual selection of sporting arms. Defending your life is a competitive activity and you cannot expect to win if either your attitude or your equipment is inferior to that of your opponent. Even thoughtfully chosen home defense guns—though suitable for urban dwellers in these so-called "normal" times—may prove inadequate under survival conditions. Perhaps the chart on the next page, which is adapted from my book *Survival Guns*, will clarify the comparison.

It should be clear from the foregoing that no one firearm is likely to be adequate for defense under the conditions contemplated here. I am, therefore, going to recommend a small battery of specialized defensive arms—each designed to cope with a specific type of tactical situation.

HOME

Members of the household who might need to use a firearm may not be motivated to become proficient in its use, or to practice often enough to retain their skill; therefore, the simplest, not necessarily the most effective, weapon is indicated.

Usually, there are no more than one, two or three intruders to deal with. Sustained rapid fire is not called for.

Time of attack is usually brief. Shots would attract neighbors or police.

Ranges are short, since, normally, you may only shoot after an intruder has entered your home.

A burglar in the home *may* not be armed or may not be armed with a firearm.

An intruder in the home is not likely to be skilled in the use of firearms. Sociopaths do not usually possess the self-discipline to become marksmen, and unless crazed or in need of a drug fix, the intruder may not be sufficiently determined to stay after meeting even the threat of resistance.

You should be concerned that any shots you fire not leave the room they are fired in, because of dangers to others in your household or neighbors, particularly if you live in an apartment house.

RETREAT

All members of a retreat group could reasonably be expected to spend the necessary time to learn how to use a number of firearms well, so the most efficient, rather than the simplest should be chosen.

If the security of your retreat is compromised at all, you will probably encounter bands of looters. Sustained rapid fire will be a probable necessity.

You may very well be "under siege" for an extended period of time, and there will be no one to help you except yourself and your immediate group.

You may encounter both short and long ranges and you can expect your assailants to make use of barriers and available cover.

Almost certainly, your attackers will be armed—perhaps very well armed, if they have robbed a military installation (a good reason for not having your retreat near one).

Looters at your retreat are likely to be well organized and extremely determined; and, probably, at least some of them will be skillful with weapons—otherwise they would not have lasted long enough to attack you! Threats will not be enough. You must be prepared to repel an attack forcefully.

In a properly planned retreat, the range and penetration ability of the shots you fire should only concern your attackers.

Rifles

Although a poor choice for urban home defense because of its excessive penetration and somewhat awkward handling in close quarters, a modern semi-automatic assault rifle should be regarded as essential retreat protection. Neither pistols nor shotguns have sufficient range, in most circumstances. Sporting rifles usually have limited magazine capacities, are somewhat slow to reload and are not designed for either the volume of fire or the abuse to which they are apt to be subjected in even a brief fire fight. City dwellers who have never been under fire often remark A) that an attack launched from several hundred yards away is not dangerous or B) that there would be plenty of time to escape and hide. I can only reply that even if the first contention were true, which it isn't, determined attackers seldom *remain* at long range if they do not encounter effective return fire; and running away— even if you were willing to do so—might not be an option allowed by your attackers. Looters tend not to be bound by the Geneva Convention.

Probably the best single choice for the purpose outlined here would be one of the better .30 caliber assault rifles chambered for the 7.62 NATO (.308 Winchester) cartridge. Such a rifle in the hands of a moderately skilled marksman is capable of almost certain hits on man-sized targets to at least 400 yards, and it is powerful enough to penetrate most body armor and chance barriers such as automobile bodies and the like. Possible choices would include the Beretta M-59, the SIG-AMT, the M1-A, the FN-FAL and Heckler & Koch's HK 91.

As a backup, one of the 5.56 (.223) semiauto rifles such as the Armalite AR-180, Ruger Mini-14 or Colt AR-15 should work out well. H&K and Valmet also produce rifles of the same general class in this caliber, but I have not had enough experience with either to recommend them. The

.223 cartridge itself is readily obtainable in quantity since it is a current U.S. military round, and in good rifles it offers excellent accuracy and reasonable stopping power to perhaps 250 yards. Recoil is practically non-existent and, consequently, the gun made to fire it can be quite compact and very light. In fact, those of you who live on ranches, farms or homesteads may find, as I have, that one of these light, handy carbines makes an excellent daily companion in either your saddle scabbard or the rack of your pickup.

Caliber .30 M-1 carbines, in my opinion, have no place in a survival battery. Although the guns are well designed functionally, the cartridge lacks both range and stopping power. A Mini-14 is just as convenient and it is both more accurate and more effective. I would also avoid pistol-caliber carbines. If you are going to carry a rifle, you might as well have the advantages that a rifle cartridge offers.

Handguns

If you are not already a skilled combat pistol shooter, becoming one should rank high on your list of survival preparations. Your defense pistol is the one arm which you can have with you at all times—even when bringing in a load of firewood, working in the garden or dragging up a freshly killed buck for butchering. It is a tool that should be chosen carefully, learned with extraordinary care and carried always, for when it is needed, it is apt to be needed emphatically and quickly.

Space does not permit a detailed analysis of all the reasons why I am going to recommend only one pistol as optimal for defense under conditions of long-term survival. If you question my choice, I urge you to read either the appropriate chapters in *Survival Guns* or Jeff Cooper's outstanding text, *Cooper on Handguns*.

Controversy over the revolver vs. the autopistol has provided much interesting reading over the years, but for our purposes, it is somewhat specious. For working gun use, revolvers have a slight edge because they save their brass for reloading instead of flinging it into the nearest underbrush, and they are capable of using more powerful ammunition for hunting or protection against large animals than most autopistols. For defense, however, I believe that the Colt .45 auto—as modified for combat by a master gunsmith—has no peer among handguns. It is adequately powerful, acceptably accurate, and reliable in the extreme. Learning to shoot it well is much easier than gaining similar competence with a revolver since one need not learn the somewhat difficult technique of double-action fire, and it is far less likely to malfunction because of hard usage or lack of routine maintenance. Further, should repairs become necessary, they can easily be accomplished from a small spare-parts kit, usually without tools, whereas a revolver in need of serious fixing requires an expert gunsmith and fairly extensive equipment. Finally, the .45 autopistol is capable of sustained rapid fire, since it can be reloaded instantly with spare magazines, and the round in the chamber is available, if needed, even while the pistol is being charged with fresh ammunition. If you are tempted to believe that this feature is unimportant, I urge you to remember that the word "looters" is plural.

Shotguns

Should your alarm systems and perimeter defenses ever be compromised and you are faced with attackers breaking into your dwelling, nothing else is as effective as a 12-gauge repeating shotgun. Although any size shot will do across a room, I greatly prefer the 12-gauge #4 buckshot loading for defense under a wide variety of circumstances.

Almost all shotguns are slow and somewhat clumsy to reload; therefore, you should choose a model with a large magazine capacity or one which is capable of being fitted with a S.W.A.T. 8 or 10-round magazine extension (Choate Machine & Tool Co., Box 218, Bald Knob, AR 72010). For me, about 20 inches of barrel seems right for close combat, but you should do some experimenting with various models and choose the one that fits you best. Probably the most efficient short-range fighting shotgun I have used is the High Standard 10B auto riot gun.[1] Its gas operation greatly lessens felt recoil, and it is designed to be used conveniently with one hand, if necessary.

Your own retreat plans and personal preferences will influence your choices from these categories, of course. If you elect a sea-going haven, for example, you may want to substitute a revolver for an autopistol in order to eliminate the hazard of empty brass on your deck, or if a land mobile approach appeals to you, particular attention should be given to folding stocks and the overall length of any defense arm you select so that it may be used conveniently from the close quarters of either a vehicle or trailer.

I realize that contemplating the circumstances under which this battery might be used will be distasteful to some readers, but I sincerely believe that, ultimately, no one can assume the responsibility for our security except ourselves. Armed Americans provide the best assurance of a free America.

Airguns

Once you have chosen your basic defense and working batteries, you may want to consider adding a few even more specialized arms to your survival stores in order to meet your particular needs, to provide some backup or the basis for improvising when necessary. In my book *Survival Guns*, I spent almost 60 pages discussing a broad range of these "special purpose weapons" ranging from combination guns and black powder arms to crossbows, yawara sticks and boleadoras. Some of them have very limited uses, but there is one that should be included in even the most modest preparations for long-term survival.

Until a few years ago, I was only casually familiar with airguns. Having grown up with the toy-like BB and pellet

[1]The 10B is no longer being manufactured; however, you can occasionally find used ones for sale.

guns designed primarily for the youth market, I tended to regard air powered arms as simply plinkers and playthings, not as serious tools. In Europe, however, where firearms restrictions have been for generations as repressive as some emotional minorities would make them in this country, airguns have been developed to a point where some of them are actually more durable, more finely made and more accurate than any firearm. Now that I have had extensive practical experience with them, I am convinced that their application to survival planning can hardly be overemphasized.

If you think that my last statement is an exaggeration, consider some of the characteristics of precision air arms which led me to make it. First, ammunition is extremely compact and inexpensive. Ten thousand pellets can be purchased for as little as $35 and that entire supply could be contained in a one pound coffee can. Further, pellets can be stored almost indefinitely and without hazard. The guns themselves are complementary to the ammunition, in that they require little maintenance and, as airgun specialists are fond of saying, they "wear-in" instead of wearing out. The better ones actually exhibit higher velocity and a smoother firing cycle after extended use than when they are new. Just how long a good one will last, I don't know, but one manufacturer asserts that his product does not even require lubrication until six million rounds have been fired.

To this extraordinary durability, fine accuracy and the low cost of shooting airguns, add the fact that many of them are virtually silent and without perceptible recoil, and you have a remarkable class of arms. But what is their practical value in a survival battery?

Although their usefulness is certainly not limited to training, that is their most obvious niche. Shooting is not like swimming or riding a bicycle. Even a master will lose the fine edge of his skill unless he practices regularly, and airguns provide an excellent means of maintaining or developing shooting skills even for apartment dwellers in the city. Bullet traps silenced with "ballistic putty" allow safe, convenient airgun shooting almost anywhere, and the fact that the guns themselves are—except for occasional local ordinances—completely free from government regulations of purchasing, ownership and transport makes them a comparatively hassle-free means of practice, especially in those areas of the country where legitimate firearms ownership and use is virtually prohibited.

Further, serious food gathering and pest control with suitable airguns are far more practical than many people realize. In fact, if you are willing to limit your targets to animals no larger than cottontails, proper air rifles will kill almost as reliably as .22s to distances of 50 yards or so. For protecting your garden from crows and other pests, destroying rodents for reasons of hygiene, or any other short range, small target shooting which must be done in and around your dwelling or barn, air rifles are just as efficient as firearms and they are considerably safer. For hunting small game, either for your table or as food for your dogs and other meat eating domestic animals, airguns are far less expensive to use and they usually destroy less edible meat than even rimfires do. They are particularly useful for squirrel hunting because of their extreme accuracy and lack of noise and they can also be helpful in routing larger pests without causing them serious harm, but use discretion here. Foxes and even larger animals have often been killed with powerful air rifles.

Just any air powered arm will not do for survival use, however. In my opinion, the spring piston guns are the design of choice for survival use. They are cocked by a single easy stroke and, since the air is compressed only at the moment of firing, their power is quite uniform. They are much more accurate and durable than any other type of airgun and many of them are very simple to repair because they use no valves or other particularly complex parts.

They are also quieter and usually more powerful than other designs and they can be virtually recoilless.

There are a number of fine spring piston rifles on the market, but I think the Feinwerkbau Sport Model (known variously as the F-12 or the F-124) is the best single choice for survival use—and by a considerable margin. It is extraordinarily durable and simple to repair, more powerful than any other rifled air arm and it is capable of a very high order of accuracy. Mine fires groups from the bench measuring .095 to .12-of-an-inch at 25 feet, and after considerable shooting it develops a muzzle velocity of 855+ fps. In normal use, only three parts can be expected to need replacement: the mainspring, the breech seal and the piston seal. It is unlikely that even these would fail in a single lifetime, barring abuse, but it might be prudent to stock two spares of each, as they are quite inexpensive.

If you would like a less costly "knock-around" gun as a backup or for your youngsters to use, the Diana 35 (sold in the U.S. as the Hy-Score 809 or the Beeman's Original) offers good quality at a reasonable price (buy this one only with a synthetic piston seal, not leather). The Weirauch models 50M and 30-S are the least expensive examples which should be considered for serious use.

Air pistols have limited application afield because their velocities are considerably lower than the better rifles and many of them are quite awkward to carry. The most convenient is the compact Webley Tempest and the very best is the Feinwerkbau F-65. Either is capable of taking small game reliably to about 25 yards and both are good for practice. For use strictly on targets, I also like the Beeman's Model 900 and the Walther LP 3, although neither of the latter two provide the simulated recoil effect of the Webley or the Feinwerkbau.

Two critical factors in selecting airguns for practical survival use are closely related: caliber and pellet choice. Although many of the better European airguns are made in both .22 and .177, the latter is the overwhelming choice of experts. Airgun pellets kill strictly by penetration in a vital area, so impact is less important than delivering the pellet to the precise point of aim with enough remaining velocity to achieve penetration. Trajectory, velocity, accuracy and range are all markedly better with the .177 caliber. Practical shooting with .22 pellets is limited to about 40 yards at most, but the .177 extends that distance to about 65 yards. Velocity is about 25% greater with the .177 and groups can be as much as 40% tighter. Finally, the cost of .177's is 1/3 less than .22's of the same design and they are more compact.

RIFLES FOR DEFENSE

A rifle—of any sort—is a poor choice for home defense under ordinary circumstances in an urban environment. For one thing centerfire rifles are unnecessarily powerful for the purpose and the unwanted penetration of even the more modest calibers can pose a serious threat to innocent parties in settled areas. Further, shoulder arms are awkward to use indoors in cramped spaces such as hallways, and they are much more easily grappled away than pistols in close encounters.

At a rural retreat or on an isolated farm in the aftermath of conditions which this column contemplates, however, a suitable defense rifle should be regarded as the single most important element in any survival battery.

If such events do occur, you are likely to encounter a superior force of armed rabble looting and burning everything in its path, and if you are to have a reasonable chance of defending yourself and your family, you are going to need more than casual arms and indifferent skills. Let's be clear on this point. Your deer rifle, a surplus GI carbine, or a menacing looking short rifle using pistol ammunition is simply not adequate under these circumstances. You will need absolutely reliable firepower at a high level—the ability to deliver disabling hits rapidly at reasonably long ranges without significant interruption. Only a modern battle rifle can provide that performance and none of them is inexpensive. You will have to weigh for yourself the probable need versus the expense of acquiring an efficient, highly specialized rifle, the sole purpose of which is to protect your life under demanding circumstances.

If you are a serious survivalist, you will doubtless consider a good assault rifle to be an indispensable purchase—as I do—even if it means a bit of scrimping or selling your color TV and taking up jogging as your sole recreation. Faced with such an important acquisition, your first consideration should be caliber.

There are really only three viable choices if your retreat is to be located in the U.S.: .30-06, .308 (7.62 NATO) and .223 (5.56 mm), and the '06 is a concession to the large number of Garands occasionally available at moderate prices. Although a fine cartridge, the .30-06 is not an available chambering in most modern *sturmgewehre*. The .308, which almost matches it in power, is a better choice for battle rifles because its thicker rim allows more positive ejection and its shorter overall length adapts it better to short actions and compact magazines. Either of the .30 calibers can provide the accuracy and power for disabling hits to 500 yards with iron sights, they offer better penetration of body armor and chance barriers (doors, barricades, automobiles) than lesser rounds and they are manageable in well-designed rifles by most adults. For these reasons, I recommend the .308 or .30-06 over the .223's if only one battle rifle can be owned by a family. The .223's have their place and we will discuss them at some length in a subsequent column, but a .30 caliber should be first on your list.

Because cost is such a factor for most of us, I have included the M-1 Garand in this discussion of .30 caliber battle rifles although it is not a true assault rifle and I consider it marginal for our purposes. It is awkward and heavy and its limited, eight-round *en bloc* clip capacity is a distinct disadvantage. It is, nevertheless, a sound and very reliable piece.

Let me interject a cautionary note at this point. I have received a good deal of mail from readers wanting to know whether semi-automatic sporters with extended magazines wouldn't serve adequately as battle rifles. Realizing the budgetary limitations implicit in those letters, I have run some fairly extensive tests to determine a realistic answer. Unfortunately, that answer is an emphatic "No!" Although there are some ersatz extended capacity magazines around made to fit some of the popular autoloading hunting rifles, I have found none that function with sufficient reliability to bet my life on. But even if suitable magazines could be fabricated, there are other problems. Sporters are simply not designed to handle the volume of fire or to withstand the abuse which may be required of battle rifles. For one thing their barrel weights and contours as well as their stocks were never intended to bear the level of heat generated by sustained rapid fire, and the generally closer tolerances of moving parts in sporting rifles often cause binding—to the point of malfunction—from heat expansion. Dirty ammunition and foreign matter in the action is also likelier to cause trouble in a sporter than in a properly designed assault rifle.

If you want to prove these facts to yourself, buy a few extra capacity magazines, take a friend along to load for you and set up at the bench of your favorite range. Fire a five-shot group at 200 yards, then fire 100 rounds through your gun as rapidly as possible. Without waiting for the barrel to cool, fire another 200-yard five-shot group—if your rifle is still functioning. The results will speak for themselves.

Next, we will consider two of the best modern .308 assault rifles produced in the world today, the H&K 91 and the Springfield Armory M1-A. They are as different as two rifles intended to fulfill similar functions could be, and one of them is almost certain to meet your particular needs better than the other.

Fewer than ten years ago, practical or "combat style" pistol matches were virtually unheard of. Now they are immensely popular. World championships are being held annually and combat pistolsmiths are so deluged with work that few of the better ones can promise a full-house combat conversion in less than a year. I suspect that practical rifle shooting with assault rifles is on the verge of a similar popularity explosion. Further, prudent, survival-oriented people have recognized for some time that a sound .30 caliber *sturmgewehre* should be the cornerstone of any carefully chosen survival battery. Yet there exists in print very little, practical, comparative data on these arms of the sort one needs to make a buying decision.

To be sure, Jane's, W.H.B. Smith and more recently, Musgrave and Nelson's *The World's Assault Rifles* provide all one could ask on the history, development and raw technical data, but few writers have addressed themselves to the questions of reliability, accuracy, controllability, ease of manipulation and repair—questions which those of us who want to buy rifles of this sort need to know. For this reason, and also in response to your mail (which is four times more frequent on this topic than on any other), I have spent the greater part of my working hours during the past two years field testing assault rifles. Among the nations of the non-communist world, there are a wide variety of 7.62x51 (.308 Winchester) battle rifles in use: the U.S. M-14, of which I consider the Springfield Armory M1-A a suitable variation, the AR-10, the Belgian FN-FAL, the Spanish CETME, the Swiss SIGs, the Italian BM-59, the German G-3 (H&K) and the Japanese Howa Type 64 (intended for reduced charge ammunition only). I have used all of them except the Howa Type 64 in the course of firing more than 14,000 test rounds.

Of the three I found most satisfactory, two are, fortunately, readily available to civilian purchasers in the U.S.

The Heckler & Koch Model 91 is a semi-automatic only version of the selective fire German G-3, and it is without question the most reliable autoloading rifle I have ever fired. No one of the three samples I have used has failed to feed or fire in more than 4,000 rounds of testing despite a mixed bag of commercial, handloaded and military ammunition—some intentionally dirty and some of unknown but obviously unpampered origins. During torture tests I even spread some cartridges with toothpaste before loading them in the H&K magazine, I dumped handfuls of dirt and twigs into the open actions and even oiled some of the cases. I fired 900 rounds at one-second intervals through one rifle, pausing only long enough to change magazines. At the end of that test the barrel was hot enough to sear flesh but I was able to keep the next five rounds in a 4-inch circle at 230 yards—and the zero had not changed measurably from the center of impact established earlier with a cold barrel.

Frankly, I was prepared for the H&K 91 to exhibit a high order of reliability, but I did not expect the level of accuracy which I found. With good ammunition, these rifles in standard—not match—grade are capable of approaching benchrest standards. Two of my test guns regularly deliver sub-minute of angle groups from the bench with one lot of U.S. military national match ammunition, and one, when fitted with the superb Zeiss Diavara scope supplied by the factory, shot into ⅜-inch at 100 yards. This performance was from untuned, out-of-the-box rifles graced with the worst trigger pulls I have encountered this side of a Mattel cap pistol.

Parenthetically, the unsatisfactory trigger action is usually uncorrectable in most assault rifles, as it is in the H&K 91. You will simply have to learn to overcome it. The curious thing, however, is that the poor trigger does not

97

seem to hamper good shooting as much as one might expect. In fact, I have been impressed with how readily a number of untrained shooters whose aid I have enlisted learned to hit reasonably small targets at unknown distances with the 91. It is an easy rifle to learn to shoot—a characteristic no doubt enhanced by its extremely light recoil.

Despite its rather awesome capabilities, there are some problems with the Heckler & Koch 91. In addition to its apparently uncorrectable poor trigger pull, the sights provided are virtually unusable. They can, however, be easily improved or replaced. The simplest expedient seems to be opening up the too small apertures with the sight broaching tool sold for that purpose by Brownells (Route 2, Box 1, Montezuma, IA 50171). If that approach doesn't satisfy you, the entire rear sight assembly can be replaced by a Williams Guide aperture, although that alternative will require the ministrations of a competent gunsmith.

Some object to the fact that the 91 does not lock open after the last shot or otherwise inform you that it is empty. If I were holding three looters at gunpoint with my last round and had to reason with one of them, I'm not sure that I would care for my action to lock open, but if you simply must have an empty indicator, I suggest that you load the last two rounds in every magazine with tracers. When you see the first red light fired, you know the last round is in the chamber and you switch magazines. Please do not write telling me that (A) tracers are not for sale or (B) that I am encouraging irresponsible people to start forest fires, because (A) much surplus .308 ammo comes from belt-packed ordnance intended for the M-60 and every fifth round is a tracer and (B) I assume that readers of this column are mature and serious people who understand that this recommendation is made only for actual combat circumstances, not plinking in the woods or target practice at the local range.

Finally, the delayed blowback system employed in the

H&K 91 makes use of ridges in the chamber which score the cases. Although this scoring is cosmetically unattractive and probably reduces case life somewhat, it does not prevent reloading. I have reloaded a number of Remington commercial cases used in the 91 seven or eight times with no failures, and trying for more than that with any autoloading rifle which may be used for serious purposes is courting trouble. I have also heard reports that some 91's eject the brass so violently that it is damaged. I have not encountered the problem, but if you do, the factory can supply a plastic deflector or you may simply remove the flange at the rear of the ejection port.

Unlike some imported arms the Heckler & Koch line is backed by superb parts and service facilities in the U.S. You will seldom need a part, because the H&K 91 just doesn't seem to break, but if you should, or if you commit the one unforgiveable sin with this rifle—disassembly without prior cocking—you can contact the sales manager, Mr. John Bressem, or his helpful service force: Heckler & Koch, 933 N. Kenmore St., Suite 218, Arlington, VA 22201. They can also supply you with literature covering the extensive line of accessories ranging from spare magazines in five to 80-round capacity (I prefer the 20s for most purposes) to bipods, .22 conversion units and even bayonets.

The .22 conversion unit, incidentally, is particularly worth consideration. It is extremely well made and simple to install. Although the chief value of this device is its utility as a trainer, it is certainly accurate enough for small game hunting and other uses as well. Even if you reload, .308 ammunition is not inexpensive and it makes so much noise that one often has difficulty finding a suitable location for practice. The conversion unit solves both problems effectively while still allowing realistic familiarization firing, since weight, functioning, appearance and trigger pull are unaltered.

Another accessory which I consider useful with most battle rifles—and a must with the 91—is the folding bipod.

It adds little to weight or bulk, but a great deal to practical accuracy.

I prefer to have both the conventional fixed plastic stock and the collapsible metal one which is quickly interchangeable, but if I had to choose only one, I would unhesitatingly opt for the latter.

If you have received the impression from this column that I am enthusiastic about the Heckler & Koch 91 and consider it a "best buy" for long-term survival use, you are completely on target. In addition to my own rather extensive tests, my personal consultation clients and readers of my survival newsletter now own more than 100 of these rifles and I have yet to receive a single complaint. In a field where such products receive extraordinary—if understandable—scrutiny and where even Mom's recipe for apple pie must prove itself, I consider that tacit testimony a remarkable endorsement.

Sometime during, or shortly after World War II, a significant number of our ranking military brass were stricken with the curious notion that individual infantry weapons ought to be capable of fully automatic fire. In order to implement this concept, we developed—and induced our NATO allies to accept as standard—the 7.62 NATO round (.308 Winchester). It duplicates the service ballistics of the .30-06 in a slightly shorter case with a thicker rim better suited for use in automatic weapons.

Almost from the day of its inception, the M-14 has been surrounded by controversy and, although it is still in use by most of our NATO troops, manufacture of the rifle has been discontinued. I will not bore you with the history of its demise except to say that, in my opinion, the M-14 was an excellent service rifle, all things considered. The basic problem, I think, with the M-14 was simply that it was capable of selective fire and, in the full auto mode, it was very difficult to handle. I have never known anyone who used one to complain about the rifle when fired semi-auto

—except of course for the weight, and no one has ever produced a rifle light enough to satisfy a foot soldier. The M1-A is essentially an M-14 without selective fire capability. Most of them, in fact, have been assembled from G.I. parts, except that the receivers are machined from investment castings of 8620 alloy, instead of forgings, and they are originally manufactured without provision for the selective fire switch.

Oddly enough, the civilian version of the M-14 has attracted a substantial amount of unwarranted criticism as well. During the past year, while I have been investigating the M1-A and evaluating test samples, I have received the following bits of misinformation: 1) M1-A's are made from welded Garand receivers, 2) the Japanese versions are better than the Italian ones, 3) only the standard grade can be considered as a practical battle rifle since the match grades are too tightly chambered for reliable functioning.

The facts are that: 1) the M1-A's are not built on Garand receivers, welded or otherwise, 2) neither Japanese nor Italian versions have ever been manufactured commercially and 3) if someone offered me my choice of the three M1-A models, I would quickly grab the heavy barrelled match grade and run, regardless of whether my intended use for it were recreational or practical.

Part of the problem here, I think, stems from the fact that *sturmgewehre* have suddenly become very popular—particularly at gun shows—and many of the buyers are generally unfamiliar with arms of this type. A gentleman of my acquaintance recently placed his latest gun show acquisition before me for an evaluation. It consisted of a welded Garand receiver fitted with a two-groove Springfield barrel and a homemade stock. He thought he had an M1-A and he had paid within $100 of the cost of a match grade. He did not. Instead, he possessed a kitchen table non-descript that I wouldn't fire by remote control from the next county.

The confusion here is probably enhanced by the fact that

ownership and location of the parent company has changed since the first M1-A's began to be produced. A large quantity of G.I. parts and virtually all of the M-14 tooling were originally sold to a firm in Texas which also acquired the name "Springfield Armory," after that military installation was closed. I have only seen and fired two examples of the Texas M1-A's, but from that experience and what I have been able to find out from M1-A buffs, these rifles are generally conceded to be among the very best of the breed. Certainly the ones I handled were superior arms in every regard from finish to function.

Further, several hundred generally similar rifles, called the Mark IV, were also assembled by AR-Sales in California. The receivers are slightly different from those produced by the Springfield Armory, however, and though their appearance is satisfactory, I have been unable to learn the details of their manufacture since they are no longer being produced.

In 1975, Reese Surplus Industries of Illinois acquired the Springfield Armory, and, to the best of my knowledge, they now produce all of the M1-A's currently offered for sale. A telephone conversation with one of the two Messrs. Reese who own the factory tends to support the confusion theory, since he confirmed that a variety of Garand type rifles ranging from ersatz BM-59's to so-called "Tanker M-1's" had been sent to them in the mistaken belief that they were all M1-A's.

Parenthetically, Reese did not laugh at the plight of these folk or imply that they would never have had a problem with his product. Instead, he commented "we try to help when we can by supplying parts or advice" and he candidly admitted that Springfield had had some problems with poor or roughly chambered barrels at the outset of manufacture. He said that these and any other legitimate manufacturing difficulties would be remedied quickly under warranty. Reese impressed me as a helpful, practical chap of the sort I would want to have handling a guarantee if I had problems.

The M1-A's were developed primarily as target rifles for civilian participation in military rifle matches and their accuracy can be of a very high order. The first group I fired from the bench with my heavy barrel match grade, using a lot of U.S. Military National Match ammunition, went into ⅞" at 100 yards. Subsequent testing with handloads produced slightly better groups with 42.7 gr. of 4895 and a 168 gr. rebated boat tail bullet. I have a custom built bull barrelled bolt action that will not do as well.

One point worth noting here, especially for survivalists, is that rifles of this type are designed to function within a very narrow range of pressures and bullet weight tolerance. Usually, that level is equivalent to military ball or match, somewhat below that of common sporting ammunition and often well below that of the heaviest factory loaded bullet weights. I don't mean to suggest that an occasional 180 gr. sporting .308 would blow up your gun, but the factory does void its warranty when ammunition other than G.I. is used; therefore, if you plan to use your M1-A extensively for hunting with factory ammunition or equivalent handloads, you would be well advised to seek advice from the manufacturer first.

I have had extensive experience with one match grade and one heavy barrel match grade rifle as well as limited exposure to three standard issue grade and two other match grades. I found all of the standards somewhat rough but serviceable, all of the match grades very accurate and the heavy barrel match grade outstanding. Functioning of my two rifles (match and heavy match) has been flawless for almost 1000 rounds each, after an initial break-in period of 100 rounds each. Because of the gas operated action, however, frequent cleaning of the bore, chamber, gas sleeve and piston are necessary to maintain reliability and accuracy. (Remember to leave the chamber bone dry after cleaning, since even a trace of lubrication can cause case setback, increasing the strain on both brass and breechblock.) Felt recoil is very light and no one strong enough to hold the rifle in offhand position should have any trouble controlling it even in rapid fire.

The flash suppressor is exceptionally effective, but its three inch length coupled to the 22″ barrel makes the M1-A somewhat more awkward in some circumstances than the H&K or the BM-59. For offhand shooting or sustained fire from a bipod, however, the balance is excellent. Most spare parts for the M1-A are readily available, usually inexpensively, since many Garand and most M-14 surplus will serve and Springfield Armory is now making a full line of accessories.

Plastic stocks are available as M-14 surplus from various sources but the M1-A's are regularly supplied with G.I. surplus walnut, new Springfield Armory beech or walnut, at the buyer's option. All use G.I. hardware including a shoulder rest butt plate, beneath which there is a recess in the butt stock for G.I. bore cleaning equipment (not furnished). The handguard is made of walnut colored fiberglass (optional).

Triggers on the M1-A are of the typical two stage military design, but they can be set up for a reasonably crisp four pound pull in the final stage and overtravel, though present, is not excessive. Sights on the match versions are too tight for my taste in practical use and should be opened up with the handy tool sold by Brownell's for the purpose.

The factory is running low on some G.I. parts and is now making their own. Upon request, however, for an additional charge, rifles will be built with G.I. parts, except for barrels in the heavy match grade. Suggested list prices are: Standard Issue Grade with G.I. wood—$535, new walnut—$567, Match Grade—$670, Heavy Barrel Match Grade—$779. If you choose an M1-A for your survival battery, I suggest that you order it with G.I. parts and only in one of the two match grades. (Weight difference between the two is only about 8 oz. and the increase is at the muzzle where it is an aid in steady holding.)[1]

THE REVOLVER AND THE AUTOPISTOL
IN SURVIVAL USE

Which would you say is better, a saw or a screwdriver? Clearly, the operative answer depends upon whether you want to cut lumber or drive screws. Even though you *could* turn a screw with the blade of a saw or separate a board with a screwdriver, neither seems particularly practical, especially if you expect to be engaged in the construction business for a protracted period.

The same sort of common sense logic should apply when considering handguns for your survival battery. Neither the revolver nor the autopistol is abstractly "better." Rather, each solves certain problems more efficiently than the other, and for that reason, each has its place in comprehensive survival planning.

Unfortunately, tired arguments from entrenched partisans have been repeated so relentlessly in firearms publications that a layman may be led to regard the choosing of handguns for practical purposes as an either/or decision between the two types of repeating actions. This sort of foolishness is further compounded in the case of some survivalists who believe that planning to improvise and get by with minimal supplies and equipment confers a special virtue unobtainable to those of us who seek every available edge against an uncertain future that careful planning may give us.

The truth is that neither the autopistol nor the revolver is, alone, entirely suitable for the wide range of frequently critical chores that a holster gun may be called upon to

[1]Dennis Reese at Springfield Armory tells me that the factory no longer makes any guns using G.I. parts. You can still find them at gun shows or on dealers' shelves but you will have to pay a premium to get one.

perform under survival conditions, and compromise in the selection of basic tools is, at the very least, unwise.

   In attempting to analyze the kinds of arms that are most likely to be required under the highly specialized set of circumstances that long-term survival might entail in the aftermath of a major disaster such as nuclear war or a socio-economic collapse, I have identified two broad categories which I call defensive guns and working guns. As those categories apply to handguns, a defensive pistol must be 1) convenient to carry on the person at all times; 2) quick to bring into action since its function is primarily reactive; 3) reliable in its function; 4) sufficiently powerful to end the threat of violence instantly from armed or otherwise dangerous human beings with a single fair hit on the torso; and 5) capable of easily controlled, sustained rapid fire in the event of attack by multiple assailants. I regard the defensive pistol as a highly specialized tool, the function of which—like a surgeon's scalpel—is so critical and demanding that one cannot also expect it to perform a variety of other tasks efficiently. A razor is not a satisfactory instrument to use for splitting logs; if it were, it would not serve for shaving.

   A working sidearm, on the other hand, must meet a far different set of requirements. In general, it should be capable of doing all of the other things a handgun might be expected to do—except excel in combat. Under actual survival conditions, the list might prove considerably more extensive, but three years of living on my ranch retreat has convinced me that a working holster gun should be expected to perform at least the following routine list of chores:

Food Gathering: The only time I seem to see wild game within shooting range is when I am *not* hunting and suitably armed with rifle or shotgun. Consequently, most of our table fare is brought to bag with the handgun I routinely wear. Since this sort of foraging is largely catch-as-catch-can, the belt gun must be capable of handling loads suitable for both the largest and the smallest game apt to be encountered in your environs. Where I live, that means anything from black bear to bullfrogs.

Pest Control: Coyotes are a distinct menace to calves, lambs and some other farm animals. Crows in your cornfield, ground squirrels in the feed bin and disease-carrying vermin such as rats, skunks, bats and some birds in your barns or near your house are considerably more than a minor annoyance under survival conditions. Better than average accuracy is called for if you expect to control these elusive pests with a pistol. Efficient shot loads may also be necessary, especially for shots that must be made near or toward your home or outbuildings.

Protection from Animals: Large livestock, especially cattle and horses, are highly unpredictable and pose a considerably greater threat than the uninitiated might believe. Even the family milk cow that may be virtually a pet can easily kill you when the mounting instinct is heightened during season, and bulls are dangerous anytime. Packs of feral dogs, already a serious danger in many rural areas, can be expected to be one of the major post-holocaust hazards. Wild animals seldom attack humans unless they are rabid, but it does happen now and then. I would be distinctly more comfortable en-countering one of the black bears that occasionally visits our blackberry bushes if I were carrying the most powerful pistol I own.

Poisonous snakes inhabit all parts of this country and, although they are not difficult to kill, they are often difficult to hit—especially if you don't see them until they are within striking distance. This is another situation that indicates a sidearm capable of handling good shot loads well.

Obviously, the foregoing recital demands versatility as the primary requisite of a working pistol. It must have a power range suitable for taking large game reliably at reasonable distances as well as small animals without destroying too much edible meat. It must provide target grade accuracy for small pests as well as reasonable trajectory for hitting such wily vermin as coyotes and foxes to extreme pistol range. Finally, it must disperse shot loads efficiently.

At this point even a novice should grasp the conclusions that this analysis of function imposes: autopistols are superior tools for defense and revolvers make better working guns.

Now, I think it is possible to justify those conclusions in an absolute sense and next month I intend to do just that by answering the traditional arguments, but for the moment let me remind you that here we are dealing with the special circumstances which might be expected in a post-holocaust environment where six shots may *not* be enough, there are no backup units or SWAT teams available if you get in over your head, your attackers don't cut and run because the police may be coming and the only gunsmith around to keep your pet equalizer perking is you.

To date, convenient and reliable autopistols do not dispose of sufficient power to make deer a certain garner at 75 yards or to stop an enraged bull before he proves you are biodegradable. They don't usually function well with extremely light or extremely heavy loads, not to mention shot charges. Revolvers do.

Revolvers are not suitable, however, for sustained rapid fire. Not only is double-action shooting difficult to master, it is also hard on the revolver. If you practice enough to become competent, your revolver will at least need periodic re-timing and it may begin to skip chambers. If you practice—as you should—with full combat loads, the cylinder may soon begin to "chatter." All of these conditions require the ministrations of an accomplished gunsmith with a full complement of specialized tools. To ice the matter, rapid fire with a revolver can be extremely dangerous. A squib load may lodge a bullet in the forcing cone or barrel and you are likely to trigger another round before you can stop, if your cadence is fast enough.

I realize that what has been said here is heresy to both camps. Never mind that it is both logical and true. I see a vision of all-purpose wheelgun fans preparing to launch missiles from a rotary pad in deepest Louisiana, and cold-eyed I.P.S.C. champions donning Adidas, baseball caps and forward rake rigs before mounting their four-wheel drives to search me out in the depths of the Pacific rain forests.

An acquaintance who is also a client and a reader of this column stopped in at the ranch recently and almost immediately thrust an accusing finger toward my not ungenerous belt line demanding, "What is *that*?" When I realized that he was not referring to my cleverly contrived modular portable food storage unit (often mistaken for ordinary body fat by the unknowing), I replied, "*That* is a stainless steel Ruger Security Six with a 2¾-inch barrel nestled snugly in a Bianchi Pistol Pocket."

"You packing a .357 wheelgun—and a snubby at that? What kind of survival retreat is this anyway?"

After my visitor recovered from the shock of finding me apparently ignoring my own advice, I explained. "At the moment, this is simply a working ranch. The balloon has not yet gone up, we are neither under siege nor do our lives depend on my bringing home some forage for table fare. In fact, deer and bear are out of season now and our obstreperous bull is at the neighbor's, so I'm not apt to encounter anything on the ranch that this little gat can't handle. I'm on my way out to check the condition of some irrigation pipe and, if I'm lucky, to eliminate a few of the two dozen or so feral cats that inhabit the back 40 before they decimate this season's quail crop. The little Ruger is light, handy and very accurate. Loaded as it is with Hydra-Shok wadcutters for the cats and a couple of Speer shot loads for barn rats and snakes, it's all I need at the moment and anything more would simply get in my way."

"But I thought you *hated* revolvers in general and the .357 in particular," my visitor replied.

"Look. Under ordinary circumstances a .357 revolver is one of the most useful general purpose handguns you could own. It can be relatively light and compact, finely accurate, pleasant to shoot with reasonable loads and it is comparatively cheap to feed with good handloads; it's excellent for small game, varmints, plinking and usually adequate even for personal defense and some aspects of police work—under certain conditions. The .357 is emphatically *not* a good first or even second choice for either a defense or a working gun in the particular environment likely to ensue from a catastrophic disruption of the social order."

"If a private citizen or even an ordinary street cop encounters armed violence now, it is unlikely that he will face more than one or two assailants. In the hands of a well-trained man, the .357 revolver is certainly adequate, if not optimal, under those circumstances. The average number of shots fired by uniformed police in such cases is only 2.4 rounds—well within the maximum speed and reliability curve of the well maintained revolver. The real problems connected with using a wheelgun for defense only begin to assert themselves when five or six rounds are not enough and reloading becomes necessary. With enough practice and a well-designed speed loader, recharging the revolver can be accomplished as quickly as one can swap magazines in an autoloader, but it is neither as certain nor as fumble free, and during the reloading sequence the revolver is completely out of service. It must be elevated to clear the empties and avoid having unburned grains of powder lodge beneath the extractor star (a condition that will completely tie up the gun). The auto needs never to be moved out of alignment with the target and a chambered round can cover or even be fired at the assailant while magazines are being changed."

"Couple these observations with the list of mechanical shortcomings applicable to the revolver in defensive use cited in last month's column, and some will still feel no pressing need to acquire a fighting autopistol. After all, the odds are long against a citizen encountering a gang of outlaw bikers in a stomping mood, and when a police officer finds himself outnumbered or outgunned, he can call in a SWAT team—and *they* usually carry autopistols in addition to appropriate shoulder arms."

"The problem is that the circumstances of a post-holocaust world—at least for the first few months—may engender armed encounters more closely resembling a battlefield fire fight than an ordinary residential instrusion or a police-felon street incident. To me, that distinct possibility demands every possible defensive edge in both skill and equipment. There can be no compromise in the selection of a survivalist's defensive arms. They must be the best and, therefore, the most highly specialized tools for the purpose, and that is especially true of the defense pistol since its tactical function is strictly that of a last resort weapon."

"The working handgun, on the other hand, may be for some more a convenience than a necessity. Presumably, if you set out to harvest game for the table or to eliminate pests or predators at your retreat, you will be suitably armed with a rifle or shotgun as circumstances dictate. That may not always prove to be the case, however, since game frequently appears when you are not specifically looking for it and shoulder arms are burdensome to carry every time you step outdoors, especially if you are working—cutting wood, mending fences or weeding the garden."

"The clear choice here is either the .44 Magnum if you reload or the .45 Colt if you do not. Moderate loads in these guns with their large diameter heavy bullets will be adequate for most of your working pistol needs. A 240 or 250-grain .44 or .45 Keith semi-wadcutter started at 850 to 1,000 feet will take deer and black bear handily out to the 50 or 75-yard range that is practical for a moderately good pistol shot and such loads are easy on the large frame revolvers chambered for them, generating no more than 10,000 to 20,000 p.s.i. of pressure. Such rounds will also take small game reliably without destroying much meat and they will put down mean livestock as well. The last couple of chambers can always be loaded to maximum levels, should they be required. These big bores also offer the advantage of distinctly more efficient shot loads and the not inconsiderable convenience of maintaining the same sight zero out to 50 yards or so whether the powder charges are light or heavy, so long as bullet weight remains the same and velocities range between 800 and 1,250 fps."

My inquisitor interrupted with a question: "If moderate loads are all you will usually need in the big bores, why not just use maximum loads in the .357 for the same duty?"

"For one thing the hottest safe load in a .357 pistol is not reliable for taking game over a hundred pounds in weight and it certainly is not a safe defense against dangerous animals. Further, no revolver made is capable of handling a steady diet of 40,000-pound-plus loads without having its useful life drastically curtailed—especially if you cannot count on the skillful ministrations of a good pistolsmith to rejuvenate it periodically. Whenever you think you need maximum loads on a regular basis in any given caliber, what you really need is more gun."

"Are you saying then that a .357 has no place in a survivalist's battery?" my visitor asked.

"No, not at all. I just don't see a prominent or essential place for it. If you are a serious survivalist, you really must have a suitably modified .45 autopistol in addition to your defense rifle in .308 or .30-06, a reliable 12 gauge repeating shotgun and a .22 rifle or two. Next on your list should be a scoped bolt action in the same caliber as your fighting rifle. Then, depending upon your particular circumstances, you might elect either a hideout or a big-bore working pistol or both. The .357 family (including the .38 Special) is so popular and ubiquitous that I would want to have something in which to fire that ammunition, if I could possibly afford to add more items to the basic battery, but I would not necessarily choose a pistol for that purpose. Either Marlin's fine new lever-action 1894 carbine or Savage's new .357/20 gauge chambering in the proven Model 24 series would be my first choice. Both of these long guns greatly increase the .357's efficiency, extending its practical range by as much as 50 percent and its game handling capability by, perhaps, 50 pounds live weight. Only then would I consider adding a .357 revolver to my list and even so I would regard it simply as a heavy duty .38, not a fragile Magnum: highly useful, but not essential. I might even opt for a good .22 pistol first."

My visitor responded, "You're really saying then that the guns which are most popular and even most useful now may be inadequate for survival use and that the popular conception of trying to choose the most versatile gun makes less sense than selecting the most highly specialized arms for the most critical tasks. If that's true, then there is not a "best" survival gun in the abstract."

"Exactly. If you want to speak of human morality or the English Lyric Poem, the word best has meaning in an absolute sense. Applied to tools, however, the term is relevant only as it applies to the function which a given tool may be expected to perform. You must, therefore, set priorities in selecting a survival battery: What shooting tasks are likely to be the most critical in a post-holocaust environment and what firearms will perform those tasks most efficiently and with the least possibility of failure. Add in the necessary requirements of long-term durability and user serviceability. Factor in your essential personal circumstances. When you do, you will probably discover that your handgun needs as a survivalist are far different from those of the casual sportsman, the household defender, the handgun hunter, the police investigator or the uniformed patrol officer. You must make these critical choices within the specific and highly specialized context of long-term survival preparedness. Do not be misdirected by the advice of non-survivalists, however well meaning, however great their supposed expertise, however extensive their experience in apparently related fields. Your life may be on the line so you must think the problems through and make your own decisions. Some expert's recommendation based on his experience in law enforcement or as a hunter, however vast, may prove to be only half-vast for you as a survivalist."

THE .45 COLT AUTOPISTOL

One of the greatest difficulties I have in writing this series is trying to condense a vast amount of serious and complicated data into one or two magazine pages each month. Since my only approach to problem solving seems to be a frontal attack with all guns firing, I tend—when something must be omitted—merely to state a summary of my conclusions and then rely on you either to deduce my reasons or else let me know in your letters that you want a more detailed discussion.

You are certainly holding up your end of our tacit bargain! In the March issue, I recommended the .45 Colt autopistol as the single best handgun choice for defensive use under conditions of long-term survival, and several hundred of you have written either to question or applaud that selection. Certainly, enough interest has been expressed to warrant some additional comment.

Before you decide that I am simply prejudiced against wheelguns and dismiss the matter, still clinging to your own bias, let me hasten to admit that I am a revolver buff. I carry a .44 Magnum daily on the ranch to deal with mean livestock, feral dogs, varmints and whatever targets of opportunity present themselves as table fare. I keep another revolver—a .45 at my bedside. For every auto I own, I have three revolvers and all of them see frequent use for hunting, informal target practice and plinking. They are flexible, useful tools for both work and pleasure but none of them is an optimal choice for defense under the conditions likely to be encountered in the aftermath of a world in disarray.

For one thing, there is the matter of maintenance. Revolvers tend to loosen and get out of time under heavy use, particularly with full loads, and it takes a high degree of skill as well as some specialized tools to accomplish some of the necessary repairs. Even when replacement parts are available and can be installed without hand fitting—which is not often—they will almost certainly need careful stoning or other precise adjustment to function smoothly. The 1911 autopistol, on the other hand, takes down completely without tools—except a screwdriver for the grip panels—and an inexpensive kit of spare parts will keep it functioning indefinitely, despite extensive use.

And the defense pistol in your survival kit should see extensive use even if it is never needed for its intended purpose. You will have to expend several thousand rounds in practice before you can realistically expect to defend your life with any handgun, particularly if your attackers are likely to be determined, well-armed and multiple. In this connection, the .45 auto offers several advantages. First, it is easier to learn to shoot well because you need not master the relatively difficult drill of double-action fire. Second, an excellent .22 rimfire conversion unit is available which allows much of your training program to be accomplished with inexpensive ammunition while still retaining the same trigger pull, balance and overall feel. Finally, the Colt autopistol will withstand the extensive shooting with full power loads that most of us find necessary for practical mastery of a big bore handgun. Any revolver that has fired a few thousand rounds in realistic combat practice will need the careful ministrations of a good gunsmith before it is placed in your ready rack.

Then there is the matter of reliability. The traditional argument here favors the revolver, pointing out the auto's reliance on perfect, full-power loads. The truth is that both arms require decent ammunition and the combat situation itself hardly calls for squibs. The supposed superiority of revolvers presumes that a faulty round will simply fail to fire and another can easily be cranked around to take its place. In fact, there is considerable evidence to the contrary. One is far less likely to encounter a faulty primer these days than to experience a stoppage because of bullets moving forward from their cases under recoil in a revolver cylinder. Further, a hang fire or a squib load which drives the bullet only part way down the barrel is much more serious in a revolver than an auto during rapid fire. Also, it has been my experience that the closely fitted working parts of revolvers are susceptible to stoppage by such minor interference as unburned powder grains and bits of congealed lubricant, lint or dust, whereas the .45 autopistol seems to ignore these petty affronts.

A good man with an efficient speed loader can reload a double-action revolver almost as quickly as an equally skilled man can change magazines in the auto, but he cannot do so as reliably, especially if efficient bullet shapes, such as semi-wadcutters, are employed, since they tend to hang up on cylinder rims. More important, the revolver is completely out of service while being recharged but the auto can fire a round in the chamber even as a fresh magazine is being inserted.

The relative safety factor—if one exists at all—between the two action types is inconsequential. Neither is safe in the hands of the untrained. When both guns are properly holstered and carried in a safe condition, neither has a significant edge in speed, so far as getting off the first aimed shot is concerned, but the recoil effect with comparable ammunition is less with the autopistol because the axis of the bore is lower, causing reduced leverage; therefore, controlled rapid fire is usually somewhat easier with it, for most people.

I regard most of what has been said up to this point as fact, since it can be verified by anyone who cares to conduct the necessary experiments, but there is one element involved in choosing a defense/survival pistol which admits at least a partially legitimate element of subjectivity, and that is the matter of "feel" or "pointing qualities." It is customary to say that whatever advantages the autopistol may possess, the revolver points more naturally. I suppose that may be true if you expect to do your shooting from the hip—or with the gun thrust forward from belt level while you squat in the so-called "combat crouch," defending your vital organs with your non-shooting arm.

Modern techniques call for raising the pistol to eye level and using both hands for support and you may find that in this stance, the auto is again superior. When you extend your arm from the shoulder and lock your wrist to provide the maximum rigid support for your pistol, most revolvers will be pointing at the sky. You will either have to unlock your wrist and turn it down or correct your revolver's heavenly aspirations with custom grips—and they may increase the trigger reach so much that you cannot acquire a proper double-action hold.

Despite occasional attempts to inject some mild humor into this discussion, I consider the choice of your defense pistol a serious matter that admits no compromise. If you remain unconvinced, I urge you to read the appropriate chapter in *Survival Guns*. If necessary, I will personally make a copy available to your nearest public library. Available from The Janus Press, Box 578, Rogue River, OR 97537 at $9.95 plus $1.00 postage.

Once you have acquired your .45 autopistol, don't expect miracles during your first session at the range. Your gun, as it comes from the box, may need some alterations so that it fits you properly and functions as reliably and accurately as it can.

It is a rare mail delivery that doesn't turn up at least one request for a "list of modifications" which "should" be made on the .45 autopistol. I have no such list and I strongly suggest that you pay no heed to anyone who does. Altering any firearm on which your life may one day depend is a serious and intensely personal business. No one but the user of such an arm—the person whose life may be on the line—should make those decisions. Even then, combat modifications should be approached thoughtfully and only after considerable experience has been gained with the particular piece to be modified.

There are at least 200 fairly common alterations which can be made on the .45 auto—all designed to increase its efficiency as a fighting arm—and I have tried most of them over the years. Based on that experience, the only absolute advice I can offer a third party is this: 1) shoot your pistol for awhile before you alter it—at least 250 rounds spread over a month—so that you have some idea of the gun's capabilities and problem areas, if any; 2) never modify a defense arm intended for survival use in such a way that standard factory parts cannot be used to make repairs; and 3) never sacrifice functional reliability to increased accuracy.

Assuming that you follow these three caveats, you can still get into some trouble unless you keep this basic premise in mind: the handgun is essentially a defensive —hence, a reactive tool, not an offensive arm. As such, it will normally come into play only after you have become aware of a threat. If it is to have any practical value, therefore, you must be able to use it with speed as well as skill. The fact that you can hit tin cans with some regularity when plinking or "keep them all in the black" on the target range does not necessarily imply that either you or your pistol require no further modifications for improvement.

A fairly realistic test of how well you and your chosen handgun might fare in a life threatening encounter with an armed adversary can easily be simulated, however. Load your pistol with full-power ammunition and hold it cocked and locked in your shooting hand with your arm fully extended, parallel to your leg, at your side. Have someone start a stopwatch and simultaneously give you the command "go." Raise the pistol to eye level, assume a two-handed hold, acquire a sight picture on a silhouette target (without visible scoring rings) placed 25 yards from you and fire five shots during a five-second time limit. If you can keep all of your shots within the confines of a ten-inch circle four times out of five, you will be a formidable opponent.

Obviously, there are two factors involved here, your skill and the suitability of your pistol, but they cannot be separated entirely. There are some modifications that can be made on a standard Colt Government Model .45 that will improve almost anyone's speed with the piece—more highly visible sights, for example. Other alterations, such as speed safeties, may not increase the quickness with which you can manipulate the piece but they may allow you to operate it more reliably when you must fire hurriedly. Still others are almost entirely subjective: some people can handle the .45 better with a flat mainspring housing or a long trigger, some with an arched housing and a short trigger. In addition to those changes that may be made to enhance speed, convenience and reliability with which the shooter can handle his pistol, there is yet another category designed to improve functioning.

Let's assume for the moment that you have recently acquired a new Colt Mark IV Government Model which you intend to use as your primary survival/defense pistol. All autopistols need some breaking in before they are put to serious use, so your first step is to fire 250 rounds or so of full-power ammunition. Next, fire ten magazines of factory hardball as rapidly as you can cycle the action and reload. If functioning was not perfect during that 70-round string, the gun should go to the factory for repairs before any modifications are made that might void your warranty.

Now that you have a reliable, well broken-in pistol, you

should spend a few leisurely hours at the range testing the accuracy from the bench. Six-inch groups at 50 yards are good enough for defensive use; four inches is about optimum. If you tighten the gun enough to shrink them much more than that, you are apt to encounter functioning problems.

There are occasional exceptions, of course. One of my pieces has been re-worked by a real master and it will shoot into two inches with good ammunition when I do my part, yet it functions better than any other autopistol I own. Do not expect that serendipitous combination, however. It is rare enough to be remarkable.

If your from-the-box .45 doesn't satisfy you on the score of accuracy, it should receive the attention of an experienced gunsmith who understands the differences between a target pistol and a combat arm. Three of the better known autopistol specialists are King's Gun Works, 1837 Glenoaks Blvd., Glendale, CA 91201; Armand Swenson, P.O. Box 606, Fallbrook, CA 92028; and Pachmayr's, 1220 S. Grand Ave., Los Angeles, CA 90015. Any of these three can make a .45 auto chew the center out of a 50-yard target with monotonous regularity, but make certain that the gunsmith you choose understands clearly that 100 percent functional reliability is more important to you than shrinking your groups the last ⅛-inch possible. Discuss the accurizing steps to be taken with your gunsmith in detail, and decide with his help whether to install a stainless match grade barrel and bushing, such as the Bar-Sto, or simply to perform the fairly routine tightening up and throating process on your issue barrel. For an autopistol to be placed in a survival battery, throating seems a good idea in any event. You can never be certain of your ammunition supply and smoothing the feeding ramp—provided it's properly done—will greatly improve your gun's ability to feed a variety of bullet shapes and materials. Let me emphasize that you may need no accuracy work at all, particularly with the Mark IV. The collet barrel bushing usually does all that is needed in this regard.

You may want to have the ejection port slightly lowered and reshaped on the Mark IV, however (it is already done on Commanders at the factory), to protect your brass for reloading. Replacing the solid recoil spring guide with a recoil buffer is also a good idea in the Mark IV, since it tends to reduce wear; but Commanders frequently fail to cycle properly with buffers.

Sights are the one modification which I feel must be made on .45 service autopistols if they are to be used seriously. The issue sights simply cannot be acquired quickly enough. Good, high visibility fixed sights will do for defense use if they can be properly zeroed, and they are somewhat less fragile than adjustable types. Properly installed and with all sharp edges rounded off, fully adjustable sights such as the Smith & Wesson K-frame revolver model, low profile Micro or Bo-Mars can be nearly as rugged and they are much easier to zero precisely if you change ammunition. Recently, I helped to design a set of fixed combat sights for King's Gun Works (the King-Tappan Combat Sights). Naturally, I like them better than anything else for the purpose, and they cost about half as much installed as adjustables. Before you cry "foul" I hasten to add that I have no financial interest in the King-Tappans.

Triggers usually need some attention on any new autopistol these days, but don't try to make them too light. A crisp let-off is desirable, but anything less than a 3½ to 4-pound pull should not be attempted. It is absolutely imperative that your hammer not "follow" or be jarred out of the sear and drop to half cock when the slide is racked on a loaded pistol, yet that is a common flaw after an inept trigger job. To test for this serious defect, lock the slide open, load one round in a magazine, insert it, point the pistol in a direction where you may safely fire and then depress the slide lock release. Try this test at least 20 times before you fire the gun and another 20 times after putting a hundred rounds through it. If the hammer drops out of full-cock even once, return it immediately to your gunsmith for correction.

For me, at least, a light, crisp pull is less important than overtravel or continued movement of the trigger after the hammer has been released. Most gunsmiths can install a flush hex headscrew in the face of the trigger that allows you to adjust trigger movement.

If you go slowly and give each modification the careful thought it deserves as you use your .45 extensively in timed practice, both you and your sidearm are likely to function more reliably under the demanding conditions of survival.

QUESTIONS & ANSWERS
Rifles

Q: As an outdoor writer myself, I take exception to your article on survival rifles. Automatic rifles of the kind you describe lack the accuracy necessary for game shooting. A good bolt action with a scope would be my choice. You also say that these guns can hit a man-sized target at 500 yards but most people can't shoot that well. B.R.H., TX

A: The "article" to which you refer was in fact one element of a three-part series (*G&A* July, August, September, 1978) specifically devoted to rifles for *defensive* use. I, too, prefer to hunt with a scoped, bolt-action sporter, but I would not care to defend my life with this type of arm.

From your letter, I can only conclude that you did not read the full series of articles and that you have never taken the opportunity to become familiar with the arms reviewed there. Otherwise, you would be aware that some of the best *sturmgewehre*, such as the H&K 91, are capable of better than ½ minute of angle groups from the bench with a scope. I have fired very few bolt-action sporters that will do as well.

Your final statement puzzles me. It is certainly true that a great many people do not shoot well enough to hit *anything* at 500 yards with *anything*. Yet some do, and it seems reasonable to me that both those who have that ability and those who aspire to it should be informed about the tools best suited for defending their lives.

Q: What's all of this stuff about semi-automatic defensive rifles? I have a bolt-action Springfield that I can make sing. In a fight, I'd match it against anybody's autoloader. Seriously, it can be fast. The butt is hardly down from my shoulder for a quick flick of the bolt before I'm cheeking it again. What do you think? J.A., PA

A: I think you'd better get a friend to hold an honest stopwatch on you before you become a legend in your own mind. A skilled man can develop a fairly high rate of sustained rapid fire with a bolt action, but with proper technique, the rifle never leaves your shoulder while you are operating the bolt.

Q: I've read your book *Survival Guns* and all of your columns in *G&A* but I'm still not convinced that the number of guns you recommend is necessary, even under survival conditions. Why not keep it simple and get a G.I. carbine (or one of the commercial copies) and a Ruger single action chambered for the same cartridge? You could buy both for less than some of the assault rifles you recommend and you only need to carry one kind of ammunition. R.H., NJ

A: Despite the fact that it is customarily fired from a shoulder arm, the U.S. .30 M-1 carbine cartridge is not a rifle class round in terms of either accuracy or power. The piece was developed during World War II as a substitute for the pistol and it was never regarded as a replacement for the battle rifle. The .30 carbine is a notoriously poor fight stopper; it offers only moderate accuracy and very limited range. On deer-sized game, it is an unreliable killer and I wouldn't want to be in the same county if it were used on bear. All of these characteristics are accentuated, of course, when the cartridge is fired from a pistol.

Q: I'm a member of a survival group that plans to join forces, if the trouble starts, for our mutual benefit and protection. Because of costs and also to simplify logistics, we want to standardize on a single rifle caliber and type for all purposes. Unfortunately, there is a disagreement among us regarding both the caliber and type of rifle to choose. Some want bolt-action, scoped sporters and others are holding out for military type semi-automatics. The majority like the .223 because it is so easy to handle, but others are holding out for the .308. We are all friends and we are all going to need each other's help during the crisis; therefore, we don't want to run roughshod over anyone's feelings by simply letting majority rule. Since all of us have read your definitive book on the subject, *Survival Guns,* we have agreed unanimously to put the question to you and abide by your decision. C.T., AZ

A: Although I appreciate your expression of confidence, it goes against my nature to hand down binding judgments that may affect the life or death of other people. If your group expects to survive a major long-term catastrophe, I suggest that one of your initial priorities should be determining how you are going to make decisions affecting the welfare of the group in the future. Neither majority rule nor following the dictates of a supposed authority strikes me as the best way for human beings to be governed. Most problems resolve themselves into self-evident solutions if you have enough reliable information and if you can eliminate emotion from the evaluation of it. Certainly that appears to be true in this case.

There are better cartridges available than either the .308 or the .223 for almost any purpose you might name, but I think you are correct in narrowing your choice to those two for long-term survival use since they are both current U.S. military issue, popular and widely available commercially, in addition to the fact that excellent sporters as well as defensive rifles of modern design and manufacture are chambered for both rounds. Optimally, I think a long-term survival battery should contain at least four centerfire rifles: 1) an especially accurate, reliable scoped bolt-action sporter in .308 for hunting deer and larger game as well as long-range aggression deterrence, 2) a highly reliable, accurate semi-automatic rifle in the same caliber with large capacity detachable magazines, designed specifically for the rigors of military use, 3) a light, compact, dependable semi-automatic .223 carbine and 4) an especially accurate .223 bolt-action or single-shot sporter for pest control. I think the versatility of such a battery will prove to be of inestimable value during the coming crisis, especially if you have chosen a fixed retreat on a farm or ranch in a small, rural community. If you *must* limit yourself to only one centerfire rifle, the clear choice would be a .308 semi-automatic of military design.

The .223 has certain valuable tactical uses and it is easier for women, youngsters, the elderly, the infirm and those of relatively small stature to handle. Unfortunately, however, the .223 is neither a certain manstopper nor a reliable killer of game, and whatever effectiveness it may possess in either category is limited to ranges of 150 yards or less. Now, please don't write and tell me that the .223 will penetrate both sides of a military helmet at 350 yards. I know that. It imparts very little shock, however, beyond 100 yards and, curiously, it is also quite ineffective at distances closer than 20 yards. So far as hunting is concerned, you *can* kill a deer with the cartridge, but not reliably—and that is neither good sportsmanship nor is it a very good survival technique.

The .308, on the other hand, penetrates chance barriers well, is accurate to extremely long range, and it is effective against human targets well beyond the distance that most skilled riflemen can hit with it consistently. It is a reasonable choice for any North American large game, although I would prefer something heavier for the large bears, elk and moose. Excessive recoil is not a factor with the .308 when it is used in one of the better modern semi-automatic military actions such as the H&K 91. In fact, overall weight seems to be more of a hindrance to the untrained than recoil effect when using such rifles. Fortunately, the muscles involved in holding a rifle in firing position are among the strongest in the body and they respond quickly to exercise and practice. Simply maintaining the rifle in offhand position with a weight of some sort, such as a heavy camera or a haversack filled with ammunition looped over the muzzle, will bring quick results. A bipod is also a big help.

Why not a precision bolt-action sporter in the same caliber instead of a semi-automatic military rifle for all-round survival use? There are several reasons. During the period of complete lawlessness, you may have to defend yourself and your retreat against mobs, semi-organized gangs of looters or even well organized paramilitary bands of outlaws, and that situation calls for sustained, controlled, rapid fire for which sporting rifles are not designed. It is a rare sporting rifle indeed that does not begin to open its groups and change its point of impact significantly when more than ten rounds are fired quickly, regardless of the type of action employed. Further, sporters tend to have smaller magazine capacities and are usually slower to reload than military rifles with detachable box magazines. With practice, a good marksman can operate a bolt and reacquire a sight picture much faster than most people would believe, but that same man can be faster still if he doesn't have to operate a bolt between shots. At 200 or 300 yards the question is probably academic, but ask yourself whether you would rather be armed with a 20-shot H&K 91 or a scope-sighted bolt action if you were being charged by half a dozen well-armed attackers who were within 50 yards of your position.

If you choose to limit yourself to only one rifle for general purpose survival use, and that choice is a proper defensive arm, at least choose one that will handle commercial, soft-nose sporting ammunition and full power reloads with suitable bullets for hunting. But, be aware that this criterion will limit your choices significantly, because many otherwise suitable arms will function reliably only with full metal jacketed bullets and only with pressures held to the relatively modest levels of military ball.

Q: I recently read your column (*G&A* April 1980) replying to C.T. of Arizona. You stated: "The .223 cartridge is limited to ranges of 150 yards. The .223 is also not a certain manstopper."

I think you are dead wrong in those statements! I am a member of the U.S. Marine Corps and have qualified twice "Rifle Expert" with the M16A1 rifle at ranges of 500 meters! I hit 9 out of 10 bullseyes!

I would not know about you, but I wouldn't like to be on the receiving end of a tumbling projectile moving at 3250 fps! I would stake my life on the .223 cartridge. C.E.H., USMC

A: I respect both your Corps and your enthusiasm for your rifle, but I think you need to take another look at your facts and your logic. First, what I said in the April column was, ". . . the .223 cartridge is neither a certain manstopper nor a reliable killer of game, and whatever effectiveness it may possess in either category is limited to 150 yards or less."

Notice I said its *effectiveness*, not its range, is limited to 150 yards or less. That you may be able to punch holes in paper with it at greater distances is not in dispute. Your comments are evidence of your marksmanship and the accuracy of your rifle, but they do not alter the fact that the .223 will not put an adversary down reliably with a torso hit, especially at long range.

Where the curious notion originated that the .223 tumbles in flight I do not know, but it's patent nonsense. If it did, you would have no accuracy at all and you would see evidence of some bullets hitting targets broadside instead of punching neat round holes. The .223 *may* tumble inside the body of someone struck with it, depending upon what anatomical structures it hits, but you can't count on it.

Finally, the 3250 fps you cite is *muzzle velocity*, which drops off rapidly. Terminal velocity at 500 yards would be piddling since the bullet has already shed more than 1000 fps at 300 yards.

The .223 is a poor cartridge for a fighting man and I sincerely hope that you will never have to stake your life on it.

Q: Why wouldn't the .223 serve as an all-around survival cartridge if loaded with soft or hollow point expanding bullets? Wouldn't it then become an adequate manstopper and/or deer rifle? My Mini-14 functions 100% with Remington soft points and they are plenty accurate. R.G., ID

A: Expanding bullets are not the panacea that some would have us believe and that is particularly true in the case of the .223. All of the expanding bullets I am familiar with in this caliber were designed for varmint or target shooting and, hence, they are highly frangible. These projectiles are meant virtually to explode when they strike even such small, thin skinned animals as ground squirrels and, for that reason, they are unsuitable either for defense or hunting deer-size game. Expansion is so quick and violent that they frequently cause only shallow surface wounds and seldom provide the penetration necessary to reach vital organs. Further, any sort of chance barrier between you and your target—even a twig—may destroy or hopelessly deflect your bullet. Until someone makes a more heavily constructed expanding bullet for the .223, your best choice for defense remains the FMJ—poor as it is.

Q: I've bought a Ruger Mini-14, equipped it with Choate's folding stock and flash hider, as you recommend, for my wife's defense gun. Now, I want to lay in a good supply of .223 ammunition, but it occurs to me that since the Mini is the only gun of that caliber in our family survival battery, we might be stuck with all that ammo and nothing to shoot it in if my wife's gun were lost, broken or stolen. Should we have a backup (cheaper, if possible)? J.N.K., NJ

A: Under survival conditions as I conceive them, it seems unlikely that you would be "stuck" with any of the most popular calibers since almost certainly there will be a great demand for common ammunition in barter. Still, it is a good idea, when planning your battery, to include at least two arms that will fire any cartridge that you might plan to store in quantity.

Your personal needs should determine the type of second gun you choose. In the case of the .223, for example, you might want another light defensive piece, an exceptionally accurate scoped sporter for predator and pest control at your retreat, or a utility combination gun for foraging. In the first category you will find nothing cheaper than the Mini-14 that will serve reliably. In the second, you might consider one of the good bolt-action light varmint rifles or the less expensive but superbly accurate Ruger No. 3 single-shot recently chambered for .223. The rugged, inexpensive and eminently practical Savage 24 is now available with a .223 rifle barrel superposed over a 20 gauge 3-inch magnum shotgun tube and that combination is one of the best choices in a utility gun for the retreat.

Q: We live on a fairly isolated farm and twice lately we have been harassed by a group on motorcycles. I have put up a chain link fence around my house, but the leader of the group said they would be back to tear it down. The sheriff says he can't do anything because he has not seen them break the law. His office is 35 minutes away, when the roads are passable. I have a pistol and a double-barreled shotgun, but I would like to have more firepower, just in case, and maybe something my wife could use. What do you recommend? G.M., CA

A: One of the good .223 semi-automatic rifles such as the Ruger Mini-14, Armalite AR-180 or Colt AR-15 and two or three spare, loaded, 20-round magazines should provide a good insurance policy in your particular circumstances. Recoil is practically nil, accuracy and stopping power are good out to a couple of hundred yards or so and all three of the guns are light, handy and easy to learn to shoot. You may also find the Mini-14 with its new, compact 10-round magazine a useful general-purpose rifle to carry around the farm on a daily basis, as I have. Varmints of one sort or another seem to crop up pretty regularly, when you live in the country.

Q: For hunting in the area where I've chosen to locate my retreat, I'm going to need a good brush gun. Ranges are very short in these woods (no more than 60 yards) and there is no game larger than deer and black bear. What do you recommend? S.T.P., WA

A: A lot of nonsense has been written about calibers that can plow through thick cover without being deflected, but the fact is that relatively little interference with the flights of any sporting round will cause it to miss its mark considerably.

I once ran some rather extensive tests on bullet deflection using rifles ranging in caliber from .17 to .45-70 and although these experiments led to no definitive answers, they did yield some interesting observations that may be helpful to you: 1. Nothing that can be fired comfortably in a shoulder arm will perform with total reliability in dense cover. 2. Round-nose bullets of at least 100 grains weight driven at a muzzle velocity of from 2,300 to 2,550 fps provide the most uniform results. Other factors such as bullet over-stabilization and distance from the target to the obstruction also have some bearing on the subject, but the configuration, speed and weight of the projectile seem to be the most telling. The best results in the tests were scored by the .270 loaded with 150-grain round-nose bullets to 2,500 fps; one of the worst records was made by the .45-70 with 405-grain factory loads—just the opposite of what you are apt to read in most articles.

The best solution, of course, is to use a combination of strategy and stalking ability so that you can shoot through a hole in the brush whenever possible. Failing that, almost any of the standard deer calibers loaded to the suggested velocity with the right bullet should give you a fair chance.

I continue to receive a significant amount of mail asking about the value in survival planning of rifles and carbines chambered for pistol calibers. Most of these queries relate to 9mm and .45 ACP arms for defensive use, and in that context I see little value in them. Even the most powerful pistol cartridges are only marginally effective when compared to the stopping power of a rifle caliber. The primary argument in favor of a pistol as a defensive arm is its convenience. If you are going to carry a rifle, then you might as well have the edge in power and range that a proper rifle caliber will give you.

That same logic does not necessarily obtain when one is considering working guns, however. The right pistol cartridge, given a boost in both power and accuracy from a shoulder arm might be just the thing for small-game hunting or short-range pest control. In particular, I like the .38 Special/.357 Magnum cartridges for such purposes. Properly loaded, they will efficiently handle table game from frogs, squirrels, rabbits and feral pigs to small deer out to 125 yards. This power range is also optimal for eliminating garden pests, feed-stealing ground squirrels, foxes, coyotes and the like at the ranges where they are usually encountered on a small farm/ranch retreat. In the past, I have had several guns modified to accommodate the .357 ranging from .30 M1 carbines to '92 Winchesters, since nothing suitable was commercially available. Such extreme expedients are no longer necessary, thanks to new model introductions from Marlin and Savage.

Having read the initial reviews based on pre-production prototypes of Marlin's .357 lever-action carbine, I hesitated to order one. Feeding problems were reported by all of the scribes I read, and photographs led me to believe that the gun was somewhat oversized for the cartridge. I waited until production models were available on dealer's shelves and then exercised my prerogative as a gun writer to order a rifle on approval. Marlin will receive a check and not a long brown package in the U.P.S.

The little carbine is hardly larger than the .22 caliber Model 39M. It is light, handy and eminently quick on target. Best of all, it shoots—far better than one has any right to expect of a piece this size chambered for this caliber. A mixed bag of .357 factory loads in a variety of bullet configurations weighing from 125 to 158 grains averaged under two inches at 50 yards for five-shot groups from the bench using the open sights provided. No feeding problems were encountered at all with either .357 Magnum or .38 Special rounds until full wadcutter .38s were tried. Even those will work through the action, however, if care is exercised.

My sample of the Marlin clearly prefers the heavier bullet weights and velocities over 1,200 fps. Speer's 140-grain jacketed hollow point performed quite well and Federal's 158-grain JSP was phenomenal. Three five-shot groups *averaged* ⅝-inch at 50 yards. I suspect that Speer's 180-grain flat point (designed for the .35 Rem.) may prove useful in handloads.

Savage, without much fanfare, continues to improve their excellent and highly practical group of rifle/shotgun combination arms, and they have lately introduced a new

Model 24 featuring the .357 over a 3-inch 20 gauge Magnum. I find this a particularly useful everyday carrying gun for the survival retreat. With it, you are prepared for virtually any sort of catch-as-catch-can pot shooting or pest control.

The rifle barrels on every Savage 24 I've ever fired are exceptionally accurate—probably because of the rigidity inherent in their superposition to the smoothbore tube— and the new .357 is certainly no exception. Five .38 Special wadcutters chewed a ragged hole at 25 yards and the Federal 158-grain JSP .357s, which proved so accurate in the Marlin, duplicated their performance in the Savage.

Although it is true that the Savage 24s are not finished like European bespoke drillings, I am hard pressed to think of anything else that comes close to their versatility and practical value at anything like their near $100 price. Better trigger pulls and more refined sights would certainly be nice, but my only substantive criticism of the 24s is that all but one model are available *only* in full choke—too tight, I think, for the all-around foraging for which these guns are designed. Still, it's relatively simple and inexpensive to polish out a bit of the constriction. If you do, you will have something very close to the optimal survival kit gun. Should you prefer a .22 combined with your smoothbore, the diminutive 24C Camper's Model is now being made with a 3-inch 20 gauge chamber combined with the rimfire and that variation has an open choke. Survivalists who have chosen a .223 defensive rifle may want to consider the newly introduced 24 chambered for that round.

Pistols

Q: I notice that you seem to place a good deal of emphasis on accuracy in combat arms but most other gun writers seem to feel that accuracy need be only rudimentary in guns of this type, especially pistols. One writer said recently in reviewing an autopistol that it grouped in 5 or 6 inches from the bench at 25 yards and that such performance was good enough for the gun's intended purpose—self-defense at close range. Is that good enough and if not, why not? S.M., CO

A: Apparently most writers in the field have considerably greater prescience than I, knowing as they seem to, that self-defense requirements will be invariably at close range, that their assailants will be fully exposed and not wearing body armor. Unfortunately, such has not been my experience.

The entire point of carrying a pistol for defense is that the need for personal protection and the circumstances under which it may become necessary cannot be known in advance. If I knew I was to be bushwhacked in the gulch, I would either stay away from the gulch or take a few friends with me and I would certainly carry more effective arms than a mere pistol.

If violent encounters in the real world were always like stand-up showdowns in the western movies, what you call "rudimentary accuracy" would probably suffice—assuming that you were using a major caliber. One or two hits almost anywhere on the torso should put your opponent down and such accuracy should be forthcoming from any serviceable pistol, at barroom distances.

What do you do, however, if someone is dragging your wife away as a hostage after a bank holdup and your best chance of ever seeing her alive again is to place a careful round in her abductor's ear at 50 feet? (A real incident, I might add.) Or suppose you are being fired upon from a doorway 25 yards away and only part of the head and one shoulder of your assailant is visible? (Another real incident.) You are camping with your wife and children in an isolated place and half a dozen armed, outlaw bikers appear, wearing flak jackets. (Bizarre as it may sound, this incident is not only true but quite recent.) The possibilities are endless.

Since the potential for such occurrences will probably be even greater under survival conditions, I consider it imperative that a defense pistol possess sufficient accuracy to allow a skillful user a fighting chance under a broad variety of circumstances. You should be able to make life uncomfortable for a sniper at, say 100 yards, or execute a head shot on an attacker wearing body armor at 50. Most of the people who really know about such things seem to agree that a pistol that will group in 4 or 5 inches at 50 yards from the bench is probably good enough. Personally, I will not carry a pistol as primary armament that I cannot shoot in 4 inches at 50 yards using two hands unsupported.

The .45 Auto

Q: Why do you put so much emphasis on customizing (especially the .45 pistol)? I'm perfectly happy with my guns just as they come from the box. I have a Diamondback that I carry on duty that is stock in every way, including grips, an S&W 39 for off duty and a Commander I keep in the bedroom. All are just as they come from the factory and I'm sure they will all serve their intended function if ever called on. I think customizing is a rip-off. J.M., UT

A: In addition to cosmetic changes, there are probably four good reasons for customizing a handgun: to make it function more reliably, to make it more accurate, to make it easier to shoot well and to make it fit the user's needs more perfectly.

Whether you choose to alter your pistol for one or more of these reasons really depends on personal considerations and shouldn't be regarded as a moral issue in any case. As your shooting skill increases or your requirements for a gun become more exacting, the more you will begin to feel handicapped by poor trigger pulls, skimpy sights, poorly shaped stocks and the like. That's the time to alter your piece—when you feel the need and know exactly what you want. In the meantime, if you're satisfied with what you have, consider yourself fortunate and spend the money you have saved by not "customizing" on practice ammo for more shooting. But don't assume that another shooter is "wrong" to make extensive alterations in his battery. His requirements or level of skill may dictate those changes.

Q: I want to get into combat shooting with a .45. I bought a Colt Government Model per your recommendation, but I've become discouraged after seeing the $800+ custom jobs that most of the shooters seem to use. I can't afford all those fancy modifications. Do you have any suggestions? J.S., CA

A: Good sights, a speed safety, an enlarged ejection port and a beveled magazine well will get you in the game. Current examples of the Government Model that I have seen are showing exceptionally good accuracy and even some quite good trigger pulls (any pistol you buy these days may need some attention to the trigger). You can have all of these basic alterations for less than $100. Whether you will need further modifications as your skill develops depends upon your individual pistol and the shooting style you develop.

Q: In planning the survival battery for my family, the choice of a defensive pistol for my son has me stumped. He is 13 and of slight build for his age but I have no doubt that he could handle a .45 auto, except—it frightens him. He enjoys shooting and I'm sure he will come around but I don't want to pressure him. Still, what do I do to become prepared now, buy him a .380 or .38 that will become useless when he has matured or get a .45 and tell him it's his when he can learn to handle it? (Initials and state withheld.)

A: At his training facility in Arizona, one of the first demonstrations Jeff Cooper performs with the .45 autopistol is controlled fire using only the thumb and one finger. That bit of showmanship almost completely defuses any reservations students may harbor about their abilities to handle a .45. Still, I think, you are correct not to push your son into accepting a tool he is not yet ready to use. Faced with your problem, I would buy my son a Colt Ace .22. It looks, functions, feels and disassembles like the .45, but since it only uses .22 ammo your son could hardly object if he enjoys shooting at all. Further, the rimfire ammo will allow plenty of practice and familiarization firing—which is probably all the boy really needs to overcome his reluctance.

If a situation occurs in which your son must use his pistol defensively, he will be at least as well off with the .22 LR as with the lesser defensive calibers such as the .380, .32 and .25. It takes substantially better marksmanship to defend yourself with a .22 than a .45 because bullet placement is far more critical, but it can be and has been done. That added measure of skill can only help your son's training.

Finally, when your boy graduates to the .45, the Ace will not become a piece of useless hardware. It is one of the best general purpose .22's on the market and I suspect it will find steady employment around your retreat for pest control and foraging.

Q: While it's still available and before prices go completely out of sight, I want to start stocking up on .45 ACP ammunition for survival, but I am bewildered by the number of different loads and bullet designs available. I also want to buy some components for handloading, and I'd like to know what you use personally for defense and hunting with the .45. G.M., WA

A: I don't sneer at any of the 230-grain jacketed factory loads for defense. I have used them all and they all give good performance, but my current favorite is the new

Frontier round that features the fine new 230-grain jacketed truncated cone bullet by Hornady. It provides both better penetration and more tissue disruption than any round nose jacketed bullet, and its functioning reliability is nothing short of phenomenal. It is also among the most accurate 230-grain factory loads, comparing favorably with two other favorites of mine—the Federal and Remington target loads (please note that the last two items mentioned, while designated "target," are loaded to full service velocity). There is also nothing wrong with the 230-grain full metal jacket round nose as loaded by Winchester. In fact, the last I heard, I.P.S.C. was using that cartridge as their standard against which to measure the loads of prospective competitors for "major caliber" classification in registered matches. If Winchester offered me a case, I would certainly take it and run, but I have used the others mentioned more extensively, and I have confidence in them.

Speer's 200-grain hollow point load would be my first choice for hunting, both because of its greater weight than the other expanding bullet loads in this caliber, and also because of its phenomenal accuracy. In some rather extensive machine rest tests I ran last year, this Speer round shot consistently tighter groups than anything else of its type when available—and out of three different .45s. From some pistols, particularly unthroated ones, the Remington and Federal 185-grain hollowpoints may offer slightly more reliable feeding, owing to their smaller nose cavities. Personally, I have encountered no functioning difficulties with the Speer round and, in any event, that characteristic would be less critical in hunting ammunition than in that intended for self-defense.

I do very little hunting with the .45 ACP, preferring for that purpose both the revolver action and the more flexible calibers for which revolvers may be chambered. Consequently, I seldom handload .45 ACP hunting rounds. For defense, I put up hard cast 200-grain semi-wadcutter bullets in carefully selected once fired cases, using 7.5 grains of Unique and applying a taper crimp to each round. I prefer Unique for general purpose pistol loads in the survival context because of its flexibility; however, some may object to the muzzle flash produced by the load mentioned, and many survival oriented shooters, for that reason, choose Blue Dot instead. With some .45 bullets Blue Dot will also produce slightly higher velocities than Unique. Good starting data for that propellant may be found in the *Speer Manual*.

Q: After years of thinking I probably couldn't handle one, I took your advice and bought a Colt Mark IV. It's great and, as you said, the recoil is just not a factor with a two-handed hold. My problem now is, what to carry it in. Could you recommend a good field holster and maybe another for combat concealment and speed. J.B.S., GA

A: Holster development has reached a very high level today and there are at least a dozen really good ones available for the .45 autopistol. For maximum protection afield, I like the lined, full-flap models by Lawrence (306 S.W. 1st Ave., Portland, OR 97204) and Bianchi (100 Calle Cortez, Temecula, CA 92390). When carrying a rifle or doing chores on the ranch, I prefer a crossdraw and the one designed by Bruce Nelson for Milt Sparks (Box 7, Idaho City, ID 83631) is the best I've seen. The fastest concealment rig I've ever used is the new breakfront "Split Second" from Survival, Inc. (17019 Kingsview, Carson, CA 90746), and for absolute concealment of a large auto, Sparks' "Mirage" ambidextrous cutaway is remarkable. A number of other makers also produce good leather for the .45, but those I've mentioned are the ones I use most often.

Q: I have a permit to carry concealed because I collect rents in what is called a "high crime area." I need something more concealable than a Colt Commander .45, but I want more punch than a .38 snubbie offers. What do you recommend? O.M., NY

A: If you are of average size and build, and if you wear a jacket, your Commander should present no concealment problems if it is properly holstered. Try Milt Sparks (Box 7, Idaho City, ID 83631) for a "Mirage" or a "Summer Special."

If you really do need something smaller, then I think the Detonics is your best bet, but be sure to get one from current production (above serial No. 4000). There has been a continuing improvement in the quality of the Detonics since it was first introduced. I've been testing one of the new ones for several months now and I'm very pleased with it. In profile it is dimensionally similar to an S&W Chief but is less bulky to carry because it is flatter.

Q: You seem to write a lot about the .45 pistol but you never mention the various .45 rifles and carbines such as the Commando and the Auto-Ordnance copy of the Thompson submachine gun. They look like a better bet to me since they have more firepower and are probably more accurate. A.R.H., NM

A: Some of the items you mention are quite accurate—especially the Auto-Ordnance—but they do not serve the same function as a pistol because they lack its convenience. They are no less burdensome to carry than, say, a Remington 870 riot gun or a Ruger Mini-14, yet they lack the decisive close range stopping power of the former and the range advantage of the latter.

The 9 mm

Q: Why do you keep writing about the need for big-bore defense pistols like the .45 when it is a well-known fact that more men have been killed with the 9mm than anything else? Are you stupid or just an a--h---? R.H.T., FL

A: Bacterial infections, automobiles and overeating have all killed more people than the 9mm and .45 combined, but it does not follow that any one of them offers optimal defense capability against an armed opponent. Cartridges in the 9mm class do not provide reliable stopping power with a single random hit on the torso; the .45 does. A wound from the 9mm may very well kill your attacker, but not necessarily before he plants flowers in your hair.

Q: Despite your negative feelings for the 9mm cartridge I want one for my survival battery and although I disagree with you a lot, you're the one writer I trust to give me the straight dope. I've been thinking of an H&K VP 70 or a PSP but I can't get reliable information about either. What do you recommend? D.E., PA

A: I don't have "negative feelings" toward the 9mm Parabellum (9x19). The evidence is simply overwhelming that it is not the best available defensive pistol round. It is quite satisfactory for a number of other uses and I would certainly rather be equipped with one in a fight than a jagged rock.

Your question raises two problems. First, both the VP 70Z and the PSP are quite new—particularly in this country—and that may be the reason why you are having trouble getting information about them. Second, your letter doesn't tell me the purpose for which you want a 9mm and that makes it difficult for me to make a specific recommendation. Fortunately, however, I have been able to examine and fire samples of both pistols extensively and perhaps a few impressions and general facts will help you make your own choice.

The VP 70Z was introduced originally in Europe for military and police use as the VP 70. With an optional shoulder stock attached, it is capable of firing three-shot bursts. The trigger mechanism is double-action only and the magazine holds 18 rounds. For importation into the U.S., the pistol was made incapable of accepting the buttstock or firing more than one shot with each pull of the trigger, and the "Z" designation was added to the model number to distinguish the semi-automatic only version.

The VP 70Z is a large pistol but quite flat and not as

heavy as one would expect. Workmanship is excellent and, although the current trend toward castings and appropriate plastics is present, the design and obvious quality of construction make their presence less blatant than is the case with many of the current military autoloaders.

Functioning has been absolutely flawless after more than 500 rounds of mixed bag ammunition, with my sample. That fact is particularly worth noting for two reasons: a) large capacity double stacked magazines often present feeding problems in some designs and b) 9x19 ammo often varies greatly in taper, rim thickness and head dimensions.

Some will have trouble with the double-action only trigger but it works well for me. It is somewhat heavy, but perfectly smooth and although the final let-off is a bit spongy, one can get used to it. Three-inch groups at 50 yards are possible from an arm rest using S&W full-jacket semi-wadcutters, but 3¾-inch was nearer the average.

The sights are my only severe criticism of the VP 70Z. Under some lighting conditions—particularly back-lighting—you simply cannot distinguish them at all. Also, the magazine release is at the bottom of the butt, European fashion, but quick magazine changes may be less important than usual in a 19-shot auto.

If you need a pistol of this sort, I think the VP 70Z is a good one, based on my brief acquaintance with it, and assuming that better sights will be added.

The H&K PSP may well be the most brilliant autopistol design since the 1911. If it ever becomes available in .45 ACP, I will probably have all of my suits retailored with special pockets to hold a pair of them. Even in 9 mm, I will be in line to buy one when these fine pistols eventually reach dealers' shelves.

The PSP is very little larger than a typical .380 pocket pistol, it recoils significantly less and yet it carries nine rounds of Parabellum when fully loaded. The sights are good, the trigger almost excellent, the workmanship is superb and my sample has fired over 600 rounds of military and commercial ammunition (including exposed lead tips and those hard to feed 90-100 grainers) without even the hint of a malfunction.

There is no conventional safety. The front strap of the grip is a lever that cocks the piece when it is squeezed in firing position. Releasing the lever uncocks it. Simple, efficient and very quick.

The bad news is availability. It may be several months before even a few PSP's are imported for sale, and even then police purchases will have priority. Large contracts to various European police and military organizations are currently receiving the factory's full output.

The H&K PSP is well worth waiting for, however, and I will prepare a full report on my tests of it in the interim.

Alternatives to the .45

Q: I read your column every month and I know you prefer the .45 auto for personal defense, but if you had to stake your life on a revolver for combat as I do, what would it be? (I'm a police officer, *required* to carry a wheelgun.) The department requires that my holster gun be a revolver, .38 caliber or larger with a barrel four inches or longer, made by Colt, S&W or Ruger. I am also required to use factory ammo only for duty.

A: Were it not for the "factory ammo only" requirement there could be several viable choices, including either the .41 or .44 Magnums. I find even the mid-range commercial loads in these calibers too hot for optimum control in rapid fire, however, and for that reason—among others—I would choose the .45 ACP S&W Model 25. It is an exceptionally well-crafted revolver and it can be reloaded quickly with ACP rounds in inexpensive half-moon clips. For your purposes, the post front sight should be reshaped to the contour of a non-snag ramp. Depending on your stature, you may want to have the 6½-inch barrel cut back somewhat. Five inches balances particularly well if you are tall enough not to find that length uncomfortable when seated.

For combat, you should practice shooting double action only and you will probably find—as virtually all accomplished DA shooters have—that the trigger should be ground smooth on its surface and substantially reduced in width. About ⅜-inch seems right in most cases. Have the gun stocked to fit your hand by a good custom maker and insist that the stocks be on the small side so that the piece cannot be easily grappled from you. Also insist that the overall contour of the stocks be flat enough on the sides so that you will have a good index of deflection.

With proper training and enough practice to learn DA shooting well, you will be considerably better armed with this pistol than the majority of your fellow officers. I have more than ordinary confidence in that particular arm, modified as outlined above. Its mate resides on my bedside table.

Q: I know you don't like .38 Specials for combat (I don't either) but that's what I'm stuck with both for my duty gun and back-up/off-duty. Please recommend a good factory load for the 4 and 2-inch .38s that my life may depend on. The department issues 158-grain round nose but allows us to carry any factory load. J.S., CA

A: For your purposes, try the Winchester-Western +P 158-grain lead SWC, catalog #W38WCP. I seldom see it on dealers' shelves, but it can be ordered for you. It is not only a very hot load with an efficient bullet shape, but for me, it also seems to shoot to the point of aim with fixed sighted revolvers—a rare phenomenon with high-performance ammunition.

Q: I know you favor big bore pistols for personal defense, but my situation is such that I *must* use either a .32 or .380 automatic. Which of the two do you prefer and what pistol would you choose? R.V.L., VA

A: Yours is a difficult and somewhat unusual problem. Ordinarily, when someone rules out serious calibers—for whatever reason—I recommend a .22 LR. Torso hits with .38 pistols, 9mms and lesser calibers have proved to be unreliable in stopping a determined opponent. One must, therefore, rely on absolutely precise bullet placement either in the brain or a major nerve plexus when using such rounds, and the ease of shooting rimfires as well as the low cost of their ammunition seems to offer the best opportunity for developing the necessary level of skill.

Since your question rules out that alternative, I can only suggest that you try to do some shooting with both the .32 ACP and the .380 ACP. There is little to choose between them objectively, but if you find you are more accurate with one than the other, opt for it by all means. If not, I'd lean toward the .380 because of the greater choice of pistols and factory ammunition available.

There are literally dozens of pocket pistols around chambered for these two calibers and they vary considerably in both quality and design. Take special note of the Walther PP and PPK's as well as the new Beretta 14-shot Model 84. There are probably no better made small autos in the world than the two Walthers, but they are somewhat handicapped for defense use by their double-action trigger mechanisms. The Beretta also has a double-action trigger, but it can be bypassed, allowing the piece to be carried cocked and locked. It is almost as large as a .45 Commander, however, and it needs more easily acquired sights.

Q: I want to buy a couple of quality .22 pistols for my survival battery. I intend for one to be an understudy for my .45 auto and the other should be small enough to carry at all times but still reliable enough to take small game out to reasonable ranges. My question is this, should I get a Colt Ace for the first use or just the conversion unit, and is there a really first class *little* .22RF for the other? R.P., GA

A: Although I have recommended and used the .22 conversion unit for years, I find the new Colt Ace notably superior on several counts. First, my sample is distinctly more accurate than any conversion unit I've ever fired, probably because tolerances can be held more closely on the Ace, since the moving parts are fitted to a specific frame, whereas the conversion unit must accommodate any receiver from a 1911 G.I. to the latest Gold Cup. Second, my Ace will fire six times as many rounds before it needs cleaning than my conversion unit can. And finally, it is simply more convenient to have a complete, fully assembled pistol than a boxful of parts that you must mount on your .45 frame every time you get the urge to rimfire.

The conversion unit, on the other hand, is extremely compact and cheaper. Both will give good service and every .45 auto owner should consider owning one or the other.

Very high quality rimfire pocket pistols are not legion, but they do exist. Two of the best are the Walthers (PPK and PPK/S) and the S&W Kit Guns. With the decline of the U.S. dollar against the gold backed Deutschemark, the Walthers seem expensive, but there are no finer rimfires of their kind made. The two models are identical except for barrel length and you should pick the one that you can shoot the best. If you prefer a revolver, the Kit Gun will not disappoint you, and it is currently being made in stainless steel, I am told, although I have not yet had the opportunity to test one.

Q: Would it be practical to handload a bullet weight comparable to your pet 230-grain .45 ACP in a .357 and would it approximate the .45 in stopping power? I am partial to wheel guns for self-defense and except for the Model 25 S&W or custom converted 28s and 27s, the .45

cartridge is only available in single actions. J.C.D., TX
A: A 230-grain slug would not be practical in the .357.
More than just weight is involved, since the bearing
surface and, hence, pressures would be greatly increased.
Further, even if you could manage to get such a projectile
out of your revolver at reasonable speeds without giving
your cylinders a hernia, remember that bullet diameter has
more influence than bullet weight on stopping power—
assuming that you have sufficient density to gain adequate
penetration.

If you insist on using a revolver for defense, the .357 will
do the job—given the right loads and enough barrel length.
On the other hand, I would certainly prefer a .44 Magnum
or .41 Magnum with full-weight Keith bullets loaded to
about 900 feet per second. Such a combination would be
more effective, easier to handle and would place far less
strain on the gun (about 25,000 CUPS for the big bore
versus some 40,000 for a full house .357).

Shotguns

Q: What about the Remington Model 870 for defense?
They don't carry much ammo and my dealer says magazine
extensions are made but are illegal. J.G.R., IL
A: The Model 870 is one of the very best pumps for
survival use in my opinion since it is both reliable and easy
to repair. I understand that the Remington factory-made
extension is not commercially marketed, but an excellent
and perfectly legal extension is supplied by mail in either 7,
8, or 10-shot configuration by Choate Machine & Tool Co.
(Box 218, Bald Knob, AR 72010).

Q: Reading your book *Survival Guns* helped me decide to
buy a 12 gauge Remington 870 for home defense and I've
added an 8-shot Choate magazine extension. A friend told

me not to bother with buckshot since #4 goose loads is all I would need. What do you think? K.M., SD

A: Range is the determining factor in selecting a shotgun load for defense. Across a room any 12 gauge shell from light skeet loads on up will do. Beyond 15 yards I would trust nothing smaller than #4 buck. From 40 yards to your maximum reliably effective range (80-100 yards) use rifled slugs and good sights.

Q: On your recommendation I bought a Remington 870 and I like it very much. Some time ago a man visiting our gun club had one with a metal folding stock on it and I have been trying to get one like it ever since to carry in my ATV where space is at a premium. I finally found one at a police supply house but they won't sell it to me. Are these gadgets illegal for ordinary citizens like me to own? If so, why and if not where can I buy one? C.J., WA

A: The folding stock manufactured by Remington for the 870 is not illegal for civilians to own or use but the last time I inquired, it was company policy to restrict both the folding stock and the magazine extension to police and military purchasers. Choate Machine & Tool Co. (Box 218, Bald Knob, AR 72010) now provides their own version of both items to the civilian market and these are very well made, functional accessories.

Miscellaneous

Q: I live in what has become a high crime neighborhood and though I feel there is legitimate reason to keep a gun at hand whenever I'm at home, I feel a little silly walking around the house with a holstered pistol on my hip and a little embarrassed going to the door that way. Can you make any suggestions about where to stash a gun so that it is out of sight, but still instantly available? L.B., IL

A: All neighborhoods are becoming high crime neighborhoods. My mail contains an increasing number of letters similar to yours and I'm afraid this society is far from seeing the peak of such a trend.

The problem with depending on a stashed gun for defense is that you have to get to where it is before you can use it, and under many circumstances that I can easily envision you may not have the opportunity. Proper doors, locks and window treatments should provide a sufficient deterrent to give you time to arm yourself, if you make a point of keeping your gun always in the room that you are occupying at any given moment. You should have an optical peephole, an intercom or both at the entrance to your home. It is simply imprudent to open your door until you know who is there. If the caller is a stranger and you still decide to let him in, it's a simple matter to slip a pistol into your waistband under your jacket or in the small of your back if you are in shirtsleeves. A second gun in a stash, either for your own use if you're disarmed, or for another member of the family, is also a good idea. One of the best devices I've found for concealing a house gun is a clever display hanger made by Mustang (28715 Via Montezuma, Temecula, CA 92390). In essence, it is an offset bent metal rod flattened and drilled for screws at one end and covered with soft plastic at the other so that it will not damage your gun when you slide the muzzle onto the rod. You simply attach the hanger to a convenient spot such as beneath the kneehole of a desk, to the back of a substantial piece of furniture placed near the wall, inside a cupboard door or on the wall itself behind a picture, TV or a stereo speaker.

Q: Our small farm/retreat is practically overrun with quail this year, but the only time I seem to see them within shooting distance is when I'm on the tractor, never when I have a shotgun in my hands. It would sure be nice to have a shot pistol that could be worn while working on the farm but the local gunshop boys tell me that such a thing would be illegal even in a single shot. You always seem to come up with ingenious solutions. Any thought on this little problem? S.A., OR

A: Since I had exactly the same circumstances on my own ranch, you can bet I gave the matter some thought and I have even come up with a solution that works well, for me at least.

Federal law restricts the transfer and ownership of *smoothbore* pistols, regardless of the type of fixed ammunition that these guns are designed to fire. The BATF doesn't seem to mind your using shot loads in your sidearm, however, so long as the barrel is rifled. A number of manufacturers have offered shot loads for revolvers, but none is potent enough for game birds at more than three feet from the muzzle. Thompson/Center, however, provides some useful barrels for their excellent single-shot pistols, specifically intended for shotshell shooting. The best of these, I think, is the .45 Colt with detachable choke. The chamber can be slightly lengthened by your local gunsmith to accept three-inch .410 shells. The choke counteracts the spin imparted to the shot charge caused by the legally required rifling and performance is all anyone could ask of the diminutive .410 from a pistol. I have taken quail and even one pheasant out to 30 yards. Similar "hot shot" barrels are provided in both .357 and .44 Magnum but I find them less suitable for the survivalist. They require specially loaded "hot shot shells"—not always easy to find—and even then their performance is closer to that of the 2½-inch .410. Despite the extended chamber, the .45 barrel handles the .45 Colt cartridge accurately, but don't forget to remove the choke before firing ball ammunition.

Q: I'm on a low budget for my survival preparations and I have to make do. A friend gave me several hundred rounds of ammo but it's all loaded with corrosive primers and I've been told that if I fire it, the priming salts may weaken the brass for reloading. Any way to salvage those cases? B.Q., OR

A: Corrosive primers will not damage cartridge brass. If these are used, normal cleaning methods will suffice. The U.S. Army procedure of cleaning the firearm for three consecutive days after firing is a good method. However, if mercuric primers are utilized in your cartridges, try this: Pull the bullets and discard the old powder charge (safely), then squirt WD-40 liberally inside each case to kill the primers. Let them sit for at least 48 hours, dry the cases and deprime them CAREFULLY with a military type depriming tool. I have performed this operation many times without incident, but a primer could still fire so take proper precautions and wear safety glasses—as you should whenever you undertake any reloading procedures.

Q: I've recently moved to Alaska to establish my retreat and I'll be flying as a bush pilot soon. I want to put together a good survival kit to carry with me in the plane at all times but I can't decide on what firearm to include. Some of the old timers here recommend a .22 rifle and others say a shotgun. I want the gun mostly for living off the land since I always carry my custom Pachmayr .45 for protection. E.H., AK

A: Alaskan fauna varies so distinctly in different parts of that magnificent state that it is difficult to know what game you might encounter without knowing the routes you fly, but one excellent choice could be the Savage Model 24C. This compact little combination gun with a .22 LR barrel over a 20 gauge is one of the most practical foraging arms I have ever used. Despite its modest price, the rifle barrel is superbly accurate and the shotgun tube greatly increases its utility. The little Savage takes down and fits snugly into its own lined soft case. For your purposes, you might pack with it a carton of high speed .22s, at least one box of high base #6s and five or ten Brenneke slugs. With those items, a good knife, some means of making fire and the materials for a good shelter, a man who knew what he was about could live comfortably for a long time in a game-rich wilderness.

Q: Will the ground walnut hulls and polishing rouge compound I use in my case tumbler harm my primers? M.T., CA

A: Never tumble loaded ammunition or primed cases. Ever!

If, on the other hand, you are asking whether traces of the residue from the polishing compound left on cases properly tumbled after depriming is harmful, I can only reply that I assume any foreign matter not belonging to the reloading formula to be deleterious and I try to remove it. Fortunately, in this instance the clean-up is easy. Just place your cases in a large Turkish towel that has been dampened with lighter fluid, squirt a bit more directly on the cases, fold the towel over and worry the cases about for a minute or two. This treatment will also remove any grease left over from the resizing operation.

Q: What's the real story on CCI Stinger .22s? I read one article that says they are better than Texas chili, another that says they are inaccurate and still another that says they won't work in imported guns. I'm thinking of putting away a large quantity of them in my survival supplies so I need to know the truth. H.C.W., NM

A: Over the past several months I have fired more than 5,000 Stingers in a variety of rimfire arms, both domestic and foreign. Based on that experience, my opinion of them is highly favorable, especially for some critical survival applications. Rimfire rifles and pistols are especially sensitive to differences in ammunition, so far as accuracy is concerned and, therefore, some guns may shoot Stingers even better than target rounds, others will not. For example, *nothing* else groups as well as Stingers in my

Savage/Anschutz Model 54, but my Remington Nylon 66 prefers Federals. Even so, we are talking about fractions. The 54 can produce ½-inch groups with them at 50 yards, the Nylon 66, 1¼-inch at the same distance. Either would do for most practical purposes within the range of the cartridge.

You ask about reliability in foreign arms and that is a rather broad question. I understand that at least two imported pistols—not chambered to U.S. SAAMI standards—can cause problems, but I have not personally encountered any difficulties. In fact, Stingers perform better in terms of both accuracy and reliability in my Walther PP, PPK and PPK/S than any other ammunition.

I would not choose Stingers for hunting edible small game with a rifle, because they tend to destroy too much meat, except with head shots. I have found them excellent for eliminating pests up to 50 pounds in weight out to 100 yards on the ranch, however, and from a pistol they are my choice for all-purpose, practical rimfire shooting. In the short gun, they are not too destructive for use on game for the pot and they are near certain eliminators of barnyard pests. If I were forced to use a .22 pistol for defense, I would load it with Stingers because at pistol velocities the highly frangible bullet holds together for superior penetration— the only factor to consider in defense shooting with a small caliber. In selecting your survival stores, add some high velocity solids or some semi-hollow points to your Stingers and you should be well supplied for any chores that you could reasonably expect your rimfire firearm to perform.

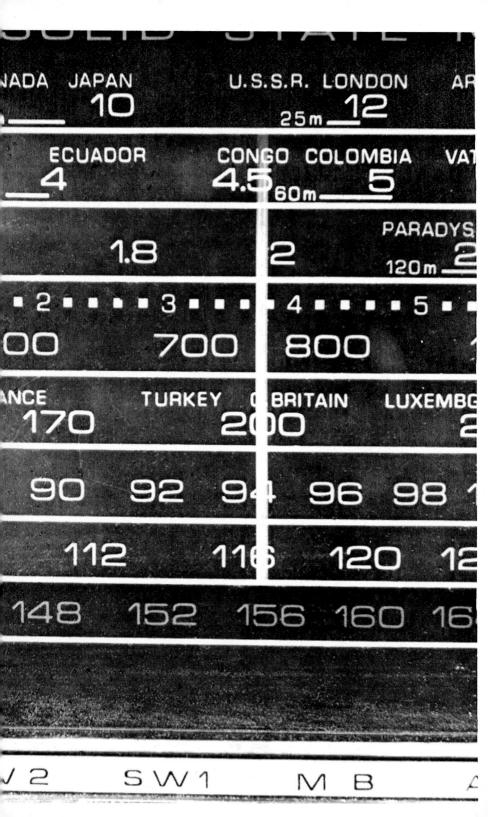

6.

COMMUNICATIONS

As you begin to implement your plans for survival preparedness and self-sufficiency, you will probably discover—as I have—that certain bonuses accrue over and above your goal of being better able to cope with an extended crisis in the future. You will find that you have increasing control over unexpected events in your everyday life, and some of the preparations which you have made against the possibility of a future breakdown in the system may save your life on an ordinary morning in the heart of the city, when the sun is shining and children are on their way to school. Earlier this year, when we were still living in Los Angeles, my wife and I had reason to be grateful for our own preparedness.

It was a typical Monday morning for us. My wife was searching for her handbag before leaving to do some errands at the neighborhood shopping center and I was dawdling over my third cup of coffee hoping that my typewriter ribbon needed changing, some pencils needed sharpening or that the phone would ring—anything to delay the little death that writers feel when starting a new piece. About ten minutes after Nancy had left, I heard the police helicopter hovering almost directly overhead and I switched on my scanner, tuning to the local air-tactical frequency. A 211 (armed robbery) was in progress and the helicopter was deploying patrol cars to block anticipated escape routes. Enough to keep me from the typewriter for a few minutes longer, but nothing out of the ordinary in a large city—or so I thought until I discovered that the location of the robbery was the bank, only a few blocks from our home, where my wife had gone to cash a check before beginning her shopping chores.

More details were being relayed on the tactical frequency: At least two men . . . well armed with shotguns and autopistols . . . hostages being taken as they entered the bank . . .

People tend to relax security measures when nothing happens for a while after they have begun to practice them and Nancy was no exception. Several times she had forgotten to turn on the car's CB radio to the prearranged frequency which we had agreed to monitor whenever one of us was away from home. I called her three times before she responded with, "wait a minute, I'm just parking in front of the bank." I told her to pull away and return home without asking any questions. There was no response.

Seconds later a voice from the scanner announced that shots had been fired and that the felons were escaping with a woman hostage. A chase ensued, the getaway car was wrecked, one of the bank robbers and the hostage were killed.

Nancy was unharmed because her response to the emergency code word I used was so immediate she had not even delayed to answer my instructions. Whatever its value in a future crisis, the radio monitoring and communications equipment we have acquired as part of our survival preparedness program has already proved its worth to my satisfaction.

This incident is by no means isolated. The CB magazines

are overflowing with reports on the use of personal two-way communications gear in emergency situations. Less dramatic, perhaps, but still valid are a number of situations related to me by clients in which their electronic survival gear has played an important role. One family was able to avoid a violent demonstration in an unfamiliar city because the scanner in their car gave them warning. In another case, a businessman escaped a devastating potential loss because he heard an important news story on shortwave hours before it was reported by the U.S. media.

I am emphasizing the immediate usefulness of these items because they can be relatively expensive to purchase and I have found that those I counsel often relegate them to the bottoms of their lists for that reason, not fully realizing their importance. A safe place, arms for food gathering and protection, a water supply and storable food are obvious survival requirements, but after those provisions have been made, priorities are less easily defined, and those which seem expensive or esoteric tend to be neglected. Under long-term survival conditions these devices may be your only source of information as well as communication, and without them you may never reach your retreat or be able to use the food you have stored or the arms you have acquired.

Just what you may need in the way of emergency radio equipment will vary considerably depending upon your individual circumstances. A couple without children living in a small town or rural area near their retreat might require nothing more than a portable, multi-band radio receiver and a pair of CB walkie-talkies.

One of my clients, on the other hand, lives in a large city where he plans to stay as long as possible, and he has three married sons living in other cities around the country. This geographically scattered but close-knit family has established a common retreat in the Pacific Northwest where they plan to meet in the event of an emergency. They keep in touch through regular "family roundtables" via ham radio, and each household has an escape vehicle prepared with elaborate communications and monitoring gear including programmable scanners, both amateur and CB transceivers as well as enough gasoline and food rations to last until they rendezvous. All of their equipment can be battery operated and, in addition, each escape vehicle carries a small, suitcase-sized generator.

Only a careful analysis of your own needs in terms of your location, the population density in your area, the size and location of your family and your own assessment of the kinds of emergencies which you anticipate can determine the optimum equipment for you, but you may find the following guidelines helpful in determining some of the specific survival uses for current state-of-the-art radio equipment.

At the very least you should have a reliable, sensitive radio receiver capable of battery operation, preferably with a self-contained antenna, which provides good coverage of the standard AM broadcast band. One of the better multi-band portables offering FM, several international shortwave bands, CB, public service, weather and whatever specialized frequencies you might need would be close to ideal. The AM band will offer official emergency information and weather reports— assuming that the stations are capable of broadcasting during the emergency—but you may profit from additional information. For example, it could be useful to know what foreign nations are saying—hence the shortwave—and it may be critical that you be able to hear police, civil defense and fire broadcasts directly.

In rural communities, small towns and other sparsely populated areas, the high and low VHF band on your communications receiver may do for this purpose, since the frequencies used are ordinarily widely separated and easy to tune, but in metropolitan areas, there is so much radio activity from police, sheriff, fire, hospital, ambulance and other public service broadcasters that most tuneable receivers cannot separate the signals, and crystal controlled or synthesized scanning monitors are needed. Most of these units can be programmed for a number of specific frequencies that you want to hear and they will either "scan" for activity or continuously monitor a selected station as you direct. If you were caught in a city during a riot or a natural disaster, being able to know where roadblocks, trouble spots or rescuers were—first hand—might save your life.

Two-way radio equipment, although designed for getting your message out as well as receiving traffic from others, is still quite valuable as an intelligence gathering tool, even if you never transmit. During the gasoline crisis I had to travel extensively but I never had trouble finding a station with open pumps, simply through listening to the exchanges from other motorists on my mobile CB. Two meter FM amateur gear will also allow you to place telephone calls from your car or a pocket-sized portable transceiver, and many hams have their cars or vans equipped with gear capable of giving them worldwide communications.

The uses for such items during a crisis are virtually endless and often critical. Even now they can provide greater convenience, safety and personal control of your life—and they can be a great deal of fun besides.

As I write this column in mid-July an interesting object lesson has just occurred for those of us who are interested in survival: New York City has suffered its second power failure in 12 years, and nothing more than a few hours without electricity has triggered a nightmare of violence there that should serve to remind us vividly that we live on the verge of chaos.

International banking establishments were closed, the major national securities exchanges failed to open, more than 3,000 arrests were made for looting, 400 policemen were reported injured, 500 fires broke out (many by arson), more than 25,000 emergency calls were placed and four times the usual number of hospital emergency cases were admitted—all because of nothing more sinister than a power outage caused by lightning striking transmission lines.

Shortly after this preview of coming attractions had transpired, I received calls from three of my clients who live in New York. Thanks to their survival preparations their lives were very little disrupted. High efficiency kerosene Aladdin lamps provided ample illumination for both security and reading, propane camp stoves cooked their meals, and dehydrated foods from their storage closets substituted for the perishables in their refrigerators.

In each case, the families involved were also able to assess the seriousness of the situation by means of battery powered monitor and scanner radios. They knew where the areas of violence were, they were saved the inconvenience—and dangers—of trying to evacuate as many others were not, and they knew that businesses were to be closed the following day, as thousands who tried to report for work did not. All three of my callers independently commented to the effect that the first-hand intelligence they were able to gain from their radio equipment had helped them cope with the emergency reasonably and without panic. Had the situation grown more serious, they would have had an edge, knowing when to leave the city for a safer place and which areas to avoid when planning their escape routes.

The most immediate intelligence during a crisis will usually be found on the so-called "Public Service Bands." These are FM frequencies allocated by the FCC to police, sheriff's and fire departments, hospitals, ambulance services, paramedics, rescue, disaster relief, the press, taxicabs, various government agencies and the like. Within this spectrum, several other important services are also included, such as: mobile telephones (152.480-152.840), the 45 channel Marine Band (156.275-157.425), the 2-meter Ham band (146.000-148.000) and the continuous broadcasts of the National Weather Service (162.55, 162.475, 162.40).

Five frequency ranges are presently in widespread use: Low Band 32-50 MHz, High Band 146-174 MHz, UHF 450-470 MHz, UHF "T" 470-512, and Government UHF 416-450. Although some multi-band tuneable radios include one or more of these frequency ranges, you may find them to be of limited value because the active channels are often so close together—particularly in metropolitan areas—that an ordinary tuner cannot separate them and all you will hear is urgent confusion. Further, you cannot move quickly back and forth between, say, the police dispatcher, a radio car and a helicopter—all of which may be broadcasting a segment of the action that you are trying to follow. These problems have brought about the development of the scanning monitor radio or "scanner," which is one of the most useful pieces of equipment a survivalist can acquire.

Briefly, a scanner is an FM receiver capable of being precisely tuned to required frequencies by means of individual crystals or a crystal synthesizer and it can be set up to scan a number of channels quickly and repeatedly, stopping only on those which are broadcasting. There are pocket models that operate on penlite batteries and are capable of covering four channels or so. Larger units designed to scan 12 or more frequencies can be had for either AC use or operation from an automobile battery.

The first scanners were crystal controlled, as are most of the presently available handheld units. Such radios may be the cheapest to buy initially and they function well enough, but in many ways they are the least satisfactory for survival use. Each channel requires a separate crystal cut for an individual frequency and the cost of these is usually between $5 and $10 each. A 10-channel, $150 scanner could cost as much as $250 when all of the crystals have been added. Further, if you travel and take your scanner with you, or if you move to a new area, you will almost certainly need all new crystals. Finally, if one of the services you wish to monitor adopts a new frequency—as they often do—or your interests change and you want to listen to a different service, you will again need new crystals.

The convenience of a handheld unit may sometimes outweigh these disadvantages, especially if it is used as a backup to a larger, more flexible model, and if you want one, those made by Bearcat and Fanon/Courier are excellent, in my opinion. Bearcat has just introduced a new handheld model, the BC-100, which is "synthesized," meaning that it needs no crystals. You punch in the frequencies you want to monitor on a calculator type keyboard and they are displayed on an LCD. The BC-100 has eight bands, search auto lockout, 16 channels and is a small 3"x7"x1½". As you would expect, it is expensive.

Bearcat, who claims the honor of having invented scanners, has just introduced a state-of-the-art model which I have been testing extensively for several weeks. An 18-channel, AC/DC unit, the Bearcat BC-210XL is programmed simply by punching in the desired frequencies by means of a front panel-mounted keyboard much like that on a touchtone telephone. A digital readout displays the actual frequency being monitored and a large, front mounted speaker provides high quality sound. The scan rate is very high—all 18 channels are sampled in ½ a second—offering an excellent probability of catching even brief transmissions. All three bands are covered with a single supplied antenna which is electronically shortened or lengthened as required. If that were not enough, the BC-210XL will actually search out unknown frequencies for activity—an extremely important feature if you should find yourself in an area where you do not know which channels are being used, or if sudden changes were made during an emergency, as they often are. Whatever scanner you finally select, don't buy until you have seen the BC-210XL.

Most stores that carry scanners will know the most active frequencies in their areas, but you should also have the inexpensive call books which are sold for various geographic areas of the U.S. In particular, you should know all of the police, highway patrol and emergency frequencies for your residence, your retreat and the jurisdictions in between.

New York's "night of violence" underlines the suddenness with which a survival emergency can surface, and for that reason I suggest that you consider the value of adding a scanner to your survival equipment without delay. One word of warning, however. Once you have sampled one of these fascinating devices, your sober, practical investment in this piece of survival gear may soon turn into a fascinating new hobby.

As the editor of a survival oriented newsletter, it's part of my job to be well informed about significant news events and trends around the world and, as I pursue this data, I am constantly amazed at how little of the really important information is even mentioned in the U.S. media, much less reported there in depth.

I am not suggesting that this state of affairs smacks of conspiracy or even that it is anything new. An afternoon in the library browsing through leading newspapers for the month preceding the crash of 1929 should convince you that the popular press may not be a sufficient early warning vehicle for impending crises. You may even find the headlines disturbingly similar to those in your current morning paper—no dire warnings, business as usual, some areas of the economy lagging but government officials and economists in agreement that things are under control with the strong measures being taken by Congress and the Administration to bring about a full recovery . . .

Short of making news gathering a career, one of the most efficient ways I know to find out for yourself what is really happening in the world is through systematic listening to a wide range of shortwave news broadcasts. If you are inclined to doubt the importance of this recommendation or its validity, try an interesting experiment. Rent a shortwave receiver for a month and listen to the English news broadcasts of at least ten foreign radio services daily, such as the BBC from London, Radio Australia, RSA from South Africa, Radio Nederland from Holland, Deutsche Welle from West Germany, HCJB from Ecuador, Radio Japan—and don't overlook the propaganda broadcasts from Radios Moscow, Peking and Havana. Make a list of the dozen or so items which you consider most significant and then see how many of them you can find covered meaningfully by your favorite domestic news source. I predict that you will never again be without a shortwave receiver willingly, and you will probably gain a new sense of urgency in making your survival preparations. At the very least, you will know a great deal more about certain far-reaching events that may dramatically affect your life, and you will have access to that information usually hours before it is reported on U.S. television, radio or in the print media.

The equipment you need for this kind of shortwave listening does not have to be very expensive, and the time required is minimal. An hour or two a day is enough once you have learned where to listen and what to listen for, but be prepared to become hooked on a fascinating new hobby. International shortwave DX-ing is one of the most interesting pursuits you are likely to encounter.

Many cheap portables purport to offer shortwave as an added feature, but usually only one small segment of the band is available or else sensitivity is poor and tuning is inadequate. A "general coverage receiver" quality multi-band portable is what you will need for serious SWL. Since this receiver will be part of your survival equipment make certain that it can be conveniently operated by batteries as well as AC current. Ideally, the radio you select should provide continuous coverage from 500 kHz to 30 MHz and have provision for receiving single sideband and CW (Morse Code) signals, as well as AM and possibly FM. About the least expensive general coverage receiver with most of these features, plus good sensitivity, is Yaesu's FRG-7, which requires an external antenna and includes a battery and car cord for DC operation. This "Volkswagen" of receivers provides better performance than some models costing twice as much.

The Panasonic RF-2000 or Sony's ICF 5900W are exceptionally good portables. They are easy on batteries and although neither features digital readout, both have dial calibration schemes that will put you within 5 kHz or better of the shortwave frequency you want. A middle of the road portable which does feature digital readout is Panasonic's RF-2900. Although the reception is equal to the other portables, this set allows exact tuning via the electronic frequency display.

TWO-WAY RADIO

Whatever your decision about shortwave listening equipment, your minimum emergency communications gear should include at least a two-way radio of some sort and a receiver capable of monitoring broadcasts from the U.S. National Weather Service, even if your interest in survival preparedness is nothing more than that of a casual outdoorsman who enjoys an occasional overnight or weekend camping, hunting, or fishing trip.

Both Ham and CB radio gear might be included if cost is not a factor, but I would select CB for survival use if forced to make a choice.

A mobile unit for your car is probably the most flexible single selection, since, with accessories, it can also be used as a base station or a battery operated portable. I consider single sideband capability a must because of its greater range and power and, fortunately, most mobile sets today have this feature. All popular SSB units provide full AM service as well as the considerable advantage of sideband when it is needed.

FCC regulations covering the 40-channel radios are so stringent that the transmitter portions of these transceivers offer virtually identical performance. There are considerable differences in the quality of the receiver sections, however, in terms of sensitivity and rejection of unwanted signals. In order to make a useful comparison, you should listen to a number of sets fed from the same antenna and played through the same extension speaker. Quality is so good, generally, among the latest 40-channel models that you can hardly make a serious blunder in selecting a mobile unit, but you will probably like the features and convenience of some more than others. In terms of both price and quality, the President Grant makes an excellent standard for comparison.

Convenient as that arrangement may be for some, others may want to consider separate handheld transceivers, and there are two which merit particular attention for survival use. The inexpensive, 100-milliwatt "Pocket Coms" are undoubtedly the most convenient and most compact CB transceivers yet devised. Their range is limited to about one mile line-of-sight in open country, but that limitation could be a blessing if you wanted to remain undetected outside of your immediate area while making necessary communications. Battery life on standby is exceptional and the units are equipped to transmit a "beep" tone for paging.

The Midland 77-861 is another widely used portable. It comes equipped with its own leather battery case and telescoping antenna as well as automobile mounting brackets and connectors. Although capable of transmitting the maximum legal power, this compact 40-channel unit has a switch permitting reduced power, when required, to save batteries or to limit transmission range.

A number of interesting accessories are now on the market which extend the CB's usefulness in an emergency, such as telephone patches that allow calls to be placed to or received from any telephone in the world, and scramblers that make transmissions unintelligible to all but similarly equipped and coded units.

Editor's Note: Grant Manning of Radio West, 2015 S. Escondido Blvd., Escondido, CA 92025, helped me update some of the recommendations in this chapter. He has just published a new catalog and I urge you to write for one. In Mel's opinion he was the most honest and knowledgeable expert on communications gear that he had ever encountered.

7.

MISCELLANEOUS

Alarms

Q: I am retired on a small social security disability pension and I live alone in an old station wagon in the Northern California mountains and National Forest areas where scores of campers are found murdered each year. I have a 12 gauge shotgun but am a heavy sleeper. There's no room in the car for a dog. Any suggestions on how I might "survive" (keep from being murdered)? L.P., CA

A: I've recently been testing a new, inexpensive alarm device that seems made to order for your situation. It's called the Night Watch Intrusion Detection System and it sells for around $75 from the Anite Co., Box 375, Pinole, CA 94564. The control box is about the size of two decks of playing cards, a single 9-volt alkaline cell (included) will operate it continuously for several months and it provides both visual and audible alerts (an earphone is included for private monitoring).

In use, you simply encircle your camp area with the almost invisible, hair-thin trip wire (8,000 feet supplied), stringing it from trees, bushes or rocks—about knee high—and then attach the loose ends to the alarm box. Anyone entering the perimeter you have established will break the fragile wire, triggering the alarm.

Were I in your position, I would certainly get one of these devices without delay, but I would also consider rearranging the station wagon to accommodate a dog as well. Then you would have a fail-safe backup to your alarm, a protector and a good companion in the bargain. For outdoor uses, the Night Watch Intrusion Detection System is not only good, but appears to be the only alarm of its type available.

Flashlights

Q: I keep a backpack loaded with emergency gear in my car. I read somewhere that to keep your flashlight from discharging you should insert one or both batteries backwards. I have a really expensive flashlight and I don't want to damage it so I thought I'd better check this advice out with you before trying it. B.A., TN

A: I have seen the suggestion to which you refer in print many times and it makes me cringe. Ordinary zinc-carbon or alkaline batteries may cause no problem in this regard, but ni-cads are a different matter.

Rechargeable nickel cadmium batteries have some interesting characteristics; among them is the ability to deliver power at a constant, undiminished rate until nearly discharged. At that point they dump their remaining power and therein lies a problem. So many instances of severe explosions in flashlights containing reversed ni-cads have been reported that battery manufacturers have begun to issue warnings.

Taping your switch in the off position is a safer means of carrying your flashlight in a pack.

H&K Emergency Kit Flare Pistol

This appealing little piece is unlike any other flare gun I have ever seen. It loads with a detachable magazine, holding five rounds, not unlike an autopistol, but *it is not a firearm* and it may be purchased currently without registration and even by mail. The flares resemble .45 ACP rounds although they are considerably larger. When fired vertically, the missiles are designed to reach a height of some 80 meters and then burn out about 20 yards before returning to ground, thereby eliminating fire hazards. They are, however, incendiary when fired directly into flammable material at close range.

The safety employed in this new design is excellent and virtually foolproof, the construction is exceptionally rugged and the workmanship is consistent with H&K's usual high standards. Recently the German air force adopted the pistol for inclusion in their pilots' emergency survival kits. If you have $99 to spare, I suggest that you order one now while you can.

Leather Care

Q: I've accumulated a lot of leather goods from following your suggestions for survival gear: holsters, slings, boots, etc. What's the best way to keep them in good shape for long wear? D.R., TX

A: Different leather items require different care. For example, you never want to soften holster leather but you must nourish it to keep it from cracking. Boots may require waterproofing and other items may need to be kept supple. All will need cleaning from time to time. There are a number of products which will do a good job, but recently I have standardized on the Original Mink Oil line—10729 N.E. Marks, Portland, OR 97220. They seem to have a specialized product for every requirement and nothing I have ever used works better.

Life Tool

The most useful survival tool is the one you have with you when you need to survive. I hope that readers of this column are beyond the stage of believing that improvising is superior to planning; however, it never hurts to consider backups to your most carefully thought out plans, particularly when such alternatives are versatile, inexpensive and convenient. I've recently been testing a little device called the "Life Tool" that meets all of those criteria. It is a thin, flat piece of steel about the size and general shape of a credit card with cutouts, holes, special purpose surface etching and sharpened edges. Among other things, it can be used as a knife, a screwdriver, a compass, a wrench, a can opener, a surface for striking matches, a nail driver, a bottle opener, a file, an insulation stripper, an entrenching tool, a signal mirror, a fishing lure, a fishhook bender or straightener, or a brush axe. The flexible Fresnel burning lens that comes with it can start a fire even on a relatively overcast day. The entire outfit, including a well illustrated instruction booklet, fits into a small plastic case that can be carried in your wallet. Get one. It's cheap insurance. Allison Forge Corp., Box 404T, Belmont, MA 02178. Price: Around $16.

Medical

Q: I belong to a survival discussion group and we are currently discussing medical aspects of retreating. Our group leader says that we should only store the medicines and instruments which we know how to use ourselves and nothing more. Do you agree? Also, we are having a hard time finding medical supplies—even if they are the nonprescription varieties. Mrs. F.R., IL

A: It is obviously wise for any survivalist to learn as much as he can about medical treatment when no physician is available, but the fact that you do not know how to suture a wound or amputate a gangrenous toe, for example, should not preclude your including sterile sutures, scalpels, hemostats and other such supplies in your kit. You may be fortunate enough to encounter a qualified person who could use such equipment if it were available, and presumably you will also continue to increase your skills both from practice and continued reading from the basic medical library that should be a part of any survivalist's stores.

Your own physician is the best place to start when accumulating medical supplies—if he will cooperate. Indian Camp Catalog contains an excellent list of non-restricted medical items from inflatable splints to sutures to splinter forceps and operating scissors (Indian Camp Supply, Inc., Box 344, Pittsboro, Indiana 46167, $1.00). Survival, Inc. (17019 Kingsview, Carson, CA 90746), sells a family "Black Bag" copied from a physician's valise, designed by Marshall Medical, which contains a blood pressure cuff, stethoscope, otoscope and other basic items together with a book—written by a doctor—describing their use by laymen. A kit of this sort can be lifesaving even now if you have a good working relationship with a progressive physician. The information which you could provide to him by phone using these simple diagnostic instruments may help him determine whether a middle of the night illness is a true medical emergency or a "take two aspirin and see me in the morning" false alarm.

I have not yet had the opportunity to examine the Marshall Black Bag and I cannot vouch for the quality of the instruments which it contains, but the concept is a good one. You will need much more in your survival medical kit, of course, and I intend to devote a column or two to the subject soon.[1]

---

[1]This was another column that Mel never got to write; he did, however, test the Marshall Black Bag and was favorably impressed.

Snakebite

Q: I am of the opinion that poisonous snakebite could be a real hazard under survival conditions, what with spending a great deal of time outdoors growing food, hunting, cutting wood and foraging. I talked to my doctor about the problem and he said that hospitalization, antivenom and life support therapy was the only satisfactory treatment. That may not be available when the crunch comes so I asked for a prescription for the serum and he said it would do no good because it won't keep.

Recently, I read in a survival newsletter I take that the suction cup devices used after cutting the fang marks was the best way, but I've also seen ads for a product to freeze the bite. Is that a cure or would you still need more treatment? R.P.G., LA

A: I agree with you about the increased risk of snakebite under post-holocaust circumstances. Until very recently, your physician's comments were correct. Nothing except first aid was available to the layman. The patient would require subsequent hospital care within a few hours at best. Further, the standard techniques of professional medical management, employing polyvalent antivenin, leave much to be desired as well because there is an extremely high rate (almost 50%) of severe allergic reaction to the serum. Even if it didn't require refrigeration and have an extremely short shelf life, this antivenin could hardly be recommended for use by laymen. Few hospitals will administer it without first testing the patient for sensitivity and the test itself frequently sensitizes the recipient, making anaphylactic shock a substantial risk.

The cut and suck technique, so popular on TV, may be effective in removing up to 50% of the injected poison *if* it is begun within three minutes of envenomation but under no circumstances should you attempt to freeze or even cool a poisonous snakebite. Although this treatment was once taught to GI's and paramedics, the increased number of amputations which resulted when the method was employed caused researchers to investigate more thoroughly, discovering that chilling actually augments the action of snake venom and gangrene frequently develops in the extremities.

After reading of a new technique for hospital management of snakebite in the *Annals of Surgery*, Vol. 179, No. 5, I got in touch with several specialists to determine whether this approach could be adapted for use by laymen under extreme circumstances. I am satisfied that it can be and I have published the rather lengthy results of this research in issue #11 of *Personal Survival Letter*. (P.O. Box 598, Rogue River, OR 97537. Single back issue price, $8.00). The advantages of this new approach are considerable. There is no risk from allergic reaction to polyvalent antivenin because none is used. It is a complete and effective therapy requiring no supportive treatment except that ordinarily involved in the healing of any puncture wound, and if the bite was not envenomated—as is frequently the case—that fact can be postively determined and treatment terminated.

The entire kit which I recommend for this procedure can be put together for $25 or $30 and kept in a fair sized belt pouch. Shelf life is excellent.

Do not be misled into believing that this method is as simple as laying on an ice pack, however. You will have to learn some basic skills that all serious survivalists should know, such as basic sterile technique, giving injections and suturing a wound, but if you have the intelligence and motor skills necessary to learn, say, practical pistol shooting, you should have no trouble acquiring the ability to manage poisonous snakebite.

Safekeeping of Valuables

Q: When I first started reading your column a couple of

years ago, it really opened my eyes. I converted just about all of my savings and cash into Kruggerands (at $149 each), as you suggested, and now with gold at almost $300 an ounce I have doubled my money. Thanks! I've worked all of my life and never had much but now, all of a sudden, I seem rich by my standards. The problem is I don't know what to do with my coins for safety. I've thought about a bank deposit box but the way things look now, I don't know how safe that would be. What should I do? R.D.W., TX

A: The first thing you should do is to consider whether you are adequately prepared in the three most essential areas of survival planning: 1. adequate arms and ammunition for defense and food gathering, 2. a nutritionally sound supply of food packaged for long-term storage and, 3. suitable shelter in a safe place. Now is the time to spend for practical goods and preparations if you have not already done so. Prices are not headed lower and significant shortages are already beginning to appear.

I think we are going to see some stunning bank failures during the next 14/18 months. Those events may not lead to a widespread, extended "bank holiday" as was the case in the thirties, but the possibility bothers me enough that I can't recommend bank deposit boxes as a worry free haven for valuables that you may need to put your hands on and run with at a moment's notice. Besides, many banks are ordinarily closed on weekends, evenings, holidays and other times when you may want access to your box. Further, once before when it was legal for U.S. citizens to own gold, the government—during an economic crisis— withdrew that right at the stroke of a pen. In an age when the government requires all banks to keep a microfilm record of the checks you write, who is to say that the banks may not suddenly be directed to list the contents of your deposit box?

If you want institutional safekeeping many cities have safety box companies that are completely unaffiliated with banks or other financial organizations and most of them are open 24 hours a day, seven days a week. Particular circumstances dictate different solutions to this problem, but don't overlook the possibility of keeping your valuables in your own hands either by installing a proper safe or developing a hiding place.

Watches

Q: I think your column is great. I've been preparing for years and it's good to know I'm not alone. You've never mentioned timepieces for the survivalist, however, and I have several questions. Is a watch an important piece of survival equipment? If so, do you get several cheap ones or an expensive one? What, specifically, do you recommend? I've heard you can use a watch as a substitute for a compass. Please explain how? S.J., TX

A: Limited, as I am, to a page or two in each issue, it will take some time to get around to all of the topics relevant to long-term survival, but yes, I consider a timepiece a valuable tool under survival conditions. Even if you are not concerned with the time of day, elapsed time and interval timing will be important. Just timing the reconstitution of freeze-dried food is fairly critical. There are several makes that will serve, but most of the time I wear a Rolex because it is extremely rugged, long wearing and dependable. Once their "superlative chronometers" have been adjusted to your personal wearing habits, they are astonishingly accurate and, more important for survival use, their rate of gain (or loss) can be predicted with such accuracy that by interpolation you could come within seconds of exact time years after setting them.

Any nondigital, accurate watch can be used as a substitute compass by holding it flat, parallel to the ground and rotating it until a matchstick or a knife blade held at the rim casts a shadow, precisely orienting the hour hand toward the sun. In the Northern Hemisphere, south lies exactly between the angle formed by the hour hand and the 12 o'clock marker, if the watch has been set to local (not daylight saving) time. There are also techniques for determining exact meridians from an accurate watch and methods for resetting your watch by the sun.

Q: I think it's outrageous that you are allowed to give brand names and addresses for products. Some of them advertise in the magazine and it's obvious you are in collusion. Unsigned

A: Every time I fail to give the source of a product that I comment on, I get a host of letters wanting to know where to buy it. I've even had a few hundred queries wanting to know where to buy my book, *Survival Guns*, even though my publisher has advertised it regularly in the pages of *G&A*. For the record, I have no affiliation with any *G&A* advertiser—except my publisher, The Janus Press—and I have never been asked by the magazine to plug a particular product. I write about what I think is important and I see nothing wrong with providing addresses for the convenience of the reader.

8.

SURVIVAL LIBRARY

Along with a bit of land in a safe place, a carefully selected battery of arms, a generous supply of storable food and seed, nothing is apt to be as valuable to a survivalist as a well-chosen library. It should be as extensive as you can make it, but it need not cost a great deal. With the broad availability of titles in paperback, good books are probably the greatest bargain you will encounter as you accumulate survival essentials.

First some general caveats. I do *not* necessarily recommend *all* of the books offered by any of the companies listed. Some titles are excellent and some are a waste of both time and money. You will need to exercise some discretion. Second, books with "Survival" in the title are not automatically what you will want to buy. In fact, most so-called "survival books" are really compendiums of tips on what to do if you become lost in the woods. I don't mean to suggest that a sound knowledge of woodscraft is unnecessary, but the subject tends to be overemphasized. Living a safe, independent and meaningful life in the aftermath of a major socio-economic upheaval bears little resemblance, in my view, to short-term wilderness survival or playing "Batman in the boondocks." You can get along nicely in this area if you study the following carefully: R. Graves, *Bushcraft*; L.D. Olsen, *Outdoor Survival Skills*; E. Jaeger, *Wildwood Wisdom*; C. Rutstrum, *New Way of the Wilderness*; B. Angier, *Survival With Style*. You may also want to add a volume or two on map and compass use such as: C. Rutstrum, *Wilderness Route Finder*; Kjellstrom, *Be Expert with Map and Compass*.

There are very few books worth having written specifically on the topic of long-term survival; however, there are a large number of good volumes on homesteading and various aspects of self-sufficiency such as operating small farms, trapping, raising livestock, veterinary medicine, basic construction and repair, using and making hand tools, as well as other "how-to" books on a variety of practical subjects. Bear in mind that the chief aim of long-term survival preparation is to become, insofar as possible, independent of the system: to provide the essentials of life for oneself without reliance upon a complex economy or sophisticated manufacturing and distribution facilities. Homesteading and self-sufficient living books are simply long-term survival texts which ignore the possibility of a hostile environment and the potential for violence. Because of that obvious shortcoming, I do not consider them to be complete guides for the survivalist, but they are, nevertheless, an essential part of a good survival library. Carla Emery's *Old Fashioned Recipe Book* (not really what the title implies, but an invaluable one-volume summary of homestead and small farm operation from milking a cow to butchering a pig); G. Logsdon, *Homesteading*; J. Seymour, *The Guide to Self-Sufficiency*; J. Vivian, *Manual of Practical Homesteading* are good examples of the genre. All of them provide useful information and some, such as Vivian's book, contain a good deal of nonsense as well. (Mr. Vivian seems not to believe in guns and thinks that one only deserves meat on the table if game is taken by primitive means.)

It is curious that few of the books devoted to living self-sufficiently in the country provide any detailed, reliable information on the kinds of guns and shooting necessary for foraging or even pest control—and none, if my memory serves, even touch on the matter of personal security. In view of the fact that I know some of the authors to be shooters, I can only conclude that they are afraid of offending potential readers whose view of nature and the back-to-the-land movement was formulated entirely from cartoon features with talking animals. If you want to balance your approach to self-sufficiency, I have no choice but to recommend my own book, *Survival Guns*, since it is the only volume written specifically about the guns, accessories and shooting techniques essential to survivalists or anyone else living on a farm or homestead in the real world.

In case you are still wondering why the survival movement has grown so rapidly in recent months and why so many writers are now beginning to deal seriously with the prospect of a near-term, man-made catastrophe, there are several useful books that you might read: Harry Browne's *How You Can Profit from the Coming Devaluation* offers an excellent, easy to understand explanation of the coming economic collapse, as does Irwin Schiff's *The Biggest Con;* Roberto Vacca's *The Coming Dark Age* offers a painstaking (if somewhat dull) analysis of why our systems—from the Postal Service to criminal justice—are breaking down; and there will soon be a new book from the Paladin Press by Bruce Clayton, which I have read in manuscript, assessing the prospects of worldwide food shortage and the possibilities of nuclear war.[1]

You will also want a reasonably complete medical library. You might begin with a simple but very useful text such as D. Werner's *Where There Is No Doctor*, the *Red Cross Handbook*, K. Sehnert's *Self-Help Medical Guide* and Eastman's *Advanced First Aid Afloat*. You should have access to more

[1]*Life After Doomsday* is available from Paladin Press, $8.95 paper, $19.95 hardcover.

than first aid techniques, of course, and the professional medical books recommended in my April, 1978 column will give you a good start.[2]

Perhaps the most frequently overlooked category of books useful to the survivalist is what might be called "post-holocaust" fiction. Even if you are not customarily a reader of novels, there are several that will provide realistic insight into the kind of world that may be facing us very shortly. Over and above these insights and the not inconsiderable factual information which many of these works contain, they are primarily valuable for the emotional conditioning that they can provide. Living through a fictional catastrophe vicariously is one of the most compelling ways of learning to cope with the stresses created by the real thing. The following list is by no means exhaustive, but it contains some of the most useful titles I have found in this category: Ayn Rand's *Atlas Shrugged*; P. Frank's *Alas, Babylon*; R. Merle's *Malevil*; J. Christopher's, *No Blade of Grass*; J. Pournelle & L. Niven, *Lucifer's Hammer*; Stein and Stein, *On the Brink*; R. Kytle, *Fire and Ice*. These volumes are not of equal literary merit, but each is interesting and although none of these presents the scenario of the collapse as I think it will occur, I have learned something of significant practical value from each.

Many of the books I've mentioned here will be available from your local bookstores or newsstands, but quite a few others will not. Further, there are scores of additional titles useful to survivalists which space prevents mentioning; if you want to start building a comprehensive survival library, therefore, I suggest that you write for catalogs from all of the following booksellers. There will be some overlapping, of course, but each offers some items that none of the others carry.

[2]See page 25.

Booksellers & Publishers

SI Equipment Ltd., 17019 Kingsview, Carson, CA 90746. One of the most comprehensive catalogs for the survivalist. Except for the self-defense books by Tegner and a couple of overpriced pamphlets, you can hardly go wrong with this list. Catalog price: $2.00

Mother's Bookshelf, P.O. Box 70, Hendersonville, NC 28791. Just about everything written on self-sufficient living and survival—good and bad—is included in this catalog . . . A "must have" reference list.

The Larder, 11106 Magnolia Blvd., North Hollywood, CA 91601. A small family business that is growing rapidly. They have some good titles and provide excellent service. Not only are they a mail-order firm, but they also have a large selection of survival books on display at their walk-in store. Catalog $1.00.

Ray Riling Arms Books Co., 6844 Gorsten Street, Philadelphia, PA 19119. This excellent and unusual firm endeavors to carry every firearms-related book in print. They are also an excellent source for out-of-print titles. I cannot ever recall their search service failing me.

Paladin Press, P.O. Box 1307, Boulder, CO 80302. Many reprints of military technical manuals as well as some useful original works. Although I was disappointed in their early "Survival" titles, they have upgraded their list and many of their self-defense books are helpful as are some on protecting one's privacy. Reliable people.

Loompanics Unlimited, P.O. Box 264, Mason, MI 48854. A broad variety of items from other publishers as well as their own. Good reference catalog ($3.00). Good service.

Ken Hale Publications, P.O. Box 395, McDonald, OH 44437. Quite a bit of overlapping with Paladin and others but some titles of his own.

Atlan Formularies, P.O. Box 327, Harrison, AR 72601. The five bound volumes of publisher Kurt Saxon's *The Survivor* are a must. He also carries other titles that he considers worthwhile.

U.S. Government Printing Office, Superintendent of Documents, Washington, D.C. 20402. One of the few things that the government does well is print informative booklets on just about every subject imaginable, including those of interest to the survivalist. Write for a catalog or pick one up at your local Printing Office branch.

Earthbooks Lending Library, Box 556, Harmony, PA 16037. This concern offers a unique service, so far as I know. You can rent any book they carry (an extensive list) for a modest fee and either return it or buy it at a discount. Good idea, good booklist and good service. Catalog $1.00.

Basic Survival Reading List*

The following is by no means a comprehensive book list on the topic of long-term survival but, taken together, the selections will give you both a good general understanding of the subject and an idea of the preparations that you need to make to insure the safety of yourself and your family.

Background
Economic

Many of these books contain recommendations for basic survival preparations, although the authors understandably focus on the financial aspects of long-term survival and tend to give the subject of personal survival short shrift.

Browne, Harry. *You Can Profit from a Monetary Crisis.* New York: Bantam, 1975. $2.25. Harry Browne has a knack for explaining economic theory in a readable, easy-to-

*Before his death, Mel had begun compiling and annotating this list, and, subsequently, I completed it, adding a few titles that were not available in October, 1980.

follow fashion. A good introduction to the economists such as von Mises and Hayek on whom he bases his work.

Friedman, Milton. *There's No Such Thing As a Free Lunch.* LaSalle, IL: Open Court Publishing, 1975. $3.95.

The German Inflation of 1923. Edited by Fritz Ringer. New York: Oxford University Press, 1969. $3.50. For you history students who enjoy finding parallels between the past and the present.

Hazlitt, Henry. *Economics in One Lesson.* New Rochelle, NY: Arlington House, 1979. $8.95. Good background if you are not familiar with the subject.

Hazlitt, Henry. *What You Should Know About Inflation.* New York: Funk & Wagnalls, 1968. $2.25. A classic.

Hazlitt, Henry. *The Inflation Crisis, and How to Resolve It.* New Rochelle, NY: Arlington House, 1978. $9.95. An up-to-date, more technical version of *What You Should Know About Inflation.*

How to Survive and Prosper in the Next American Depression, War or Revolution. San Diego: Financial Management Associates, 1978. $14.95. Excellent explanation of how we arrived at the brink.

Myers, C.V. *The Coming Deflation, It's Dangers and Opportunities.* New York: Arlington House, 1976. $9.95. Unlike some economists who foresee an economic collapse Myers realizes that violence will be one of its corollaries.

Ruff, Howard. *How to Prosper During the Coming Bad Years.* New York: Warner Books, 1980. $2.75. Part I is a readable popular treatment of the problems covered in a more scholarly fashion by other authors on this list.

Vacca, Roberto. (Translated by J.S. Whale from the Italian). *The Coming Dark Age*. New York: Doubleday/ Anchor, 1974. $2.50. Analysis of why our systems are breaking down.

Government
If you haven't done so already, write your Congressman for copies of the International Emergency Powers Act of 1977 and its companion legislation entitled Executive Order 11490, Public Law 96-221 and H.R. 4628. (See pages 5-7 for a description of these bills.)

Schiff, Irwin. *The Biggest Con, How the Government Is Fleecing You*. Hamden, CT: Freedom Books, 1977. $5.95. Well researched and documented exposé of government fraud, deception, and bankruptcy. Must reading.

Military
Crozier, Brian. *Strategy of Survival*. New York: Arlington House, 1978. $8.95. Using excellent maps and charts, the author explains how and why we have been fighting—and losing—the "Third World War" since 1944.

Douglass, Joseph D., and Amoretta M. Hoeber. *Soviet Strategy for Nuclear War*. (Ed. by Richard F. Staar.) Stanford, CA: Hoover Institution Press, 1979. $5.95. A brilliant and sobering analysis of Soviet military doctrine. Do yourself a favor and read this book.

Speed, Roger D. *Strategic Deterrence in the 1980's*. Stanford, CA: Hoover Institution Press, 1979. $7.95. Technical discussion of the vulnerability of U.S. strategic forces.

Walt, Lewis W., Gen., USMC (ret.). *The Eleventh Hour*. Ottawa, IL: Caroline House, 1979. $9.95. As Eugene Rostow says in the Foreword, this is a "calm, reasoned and realistic appraisal of our strategic situation." The most readable and least technical of the books dealing with our military status.

Other

McKeever, Jim. *Christians Will Go Through the Tribulation and How to Prepare for It.* Medford, OR: Alpha Omega Publishing Co., 1978. $5.95. Useful introduction to the topic for those who will only heed warnings based on Biblical interpretation.

McMaster, R.E., Jr. *Cycles of War: The Next Six Years.* Whitefish, MT: L. McMaster Publishing, 1978. $11.00. A look at the various economic, political, psychological, climate and warfare cycles and the way in which they all point to the early 1980's as years of crisis.

Toffler, Alvin. *The Eco-Spasm Report, Why Our Economy Is Running Out of Control.* New York: Bantam, 1975. $1.75. Brilliant scenarios of the coming collapse although Mel totally disagreed with the author's solutions. Out-of-print but can still be found in stores with a large selection of paperbacks.

Toffler, Alvin. *The Third Wave.* New York: Bantam, 1980. $3.95. A provocative and readable look at the social and economic upheavals facing us. Survivalists are "Third Wave" people.

Changes in the earth's weather patterns and overpopulation are not only problems in themselves but are certain to aggravate any crisis brought about by a socio-economic collapse, a dictatorship or a war. The titles listed are but two of the many current books on both subjects.

Borgstrom, Georg. *The Hungry Planet: The Modern World at the Edge of Famine.* 2nd rev. ed. New York: MacMillan, 1972. $3.95. The dangers of overpopulation.

Ponte, Lowell. *The Cooling.* Englewood Cliffs, NJ: Prentice-Hall, 1976. $8.95. All about the coming Ice Age.

Preparation
Psychological
Perhaps the best way to prepare yourself emotionally for the stresses in a post-holocaust world is to experience them vicariously by reading as many of the titles listed below as you can find.

Budrys, Algis. *Some Will Not Die.* (Ed. by Polly and Kelly Freas.) Donning Co., 1978. $4.95.

Cameron, Kenneth M. *Power Play.* New York: Popular Library, 1979. $2.25.

Christopher, John. *No Blade of Grass.* New York: Avon Books, 1980. $1.95.

Erdman, Paul. *The Crash of '79.* New York: Simon & Schuster, 1977. $2.75.

Erdman, Paul. *The Last Days of America.* New York: Simon & Schuster, 1981. $13.95.

Frank, Pat. *Alas, Babylon.* New York: Bantam Books, 1976. $2.25.

Hackett, Gen. Sir John, and other top-ranking NATO generals and advisors. *The Third World War—August 1985.* New York: MacMillan, 1979. $12.95.

Kytle, Ray. *Fire and Ice.* New York: David McKay, 1975. $7.95. Out-of-print. Try science-fiction bookstores or the library.

Lange, Oliver. *Vandenberg.* New York: Stein & Day, 1971. Out-of-print but well worth trying to locate. Chilling descriptions of life in a U.S. occupied by Soviet troops.

Merle, Robert. *Malevil.* New York: Warner Books, 1975. $1.95.

Niven, Larry, and Jerry Pournelle. *Lucifer's Hammer.* New York: Fawcett Crest, 1979. $2.50.

Rand, Ayn. *Atlas Shrugged*. New York: Signet Books (New American Library of World Literature, Inc.), 1970. $3.50. If you haven't read this prophetic work, do so. Ayn Rand wrote it in 1957 and 23 years later her vision of the future has, for the most part, become reality.

Schulman, J. Neil. *Alongside Night*. New York: Crown Publishers, 1979. $8.95.

Stein, Benjamin and Herbert. *On the Brink*. New York: Ballantine, 1978. $1.95.

Terman, Douglas. *Free Flight*. New York: Charles Scribner's Sons, 1980. $11.95.

General
Only during the last year have any books appeared that are devoted specifically to long-term survival preparations; consequently, this section is quite brief. For space reasons, I have not included the many excellent books on homesteading and various other aspects of self-sufficiency.

Bergman, Mary. *Survival Family*. Salt Lake City: Hawkes Publishing, 1977. $3.95. If you want to know what it would be like to live independently of the system, read this account of a year in the life of a Utah family, which existed without electricity, phones, or any other utilities—and enjoyed it.

Clayton, Bruce. *Life After Doomsday*. Boulder, CO: Paladin Press, 1980. $19.95. Must reading. Excellent material on building and equipping a shelter that will protect you from a nuclear blast. Good maps and charts of fallout, hurricane and earthquake patterns.

Clayton, Bruce. *Survival Books 1981*. Los Angeles: Media West, 1981. $14.95. Available from the distributor,

S.I. (see information on page 185). Before buying a host of books, I suggest that you buy this book and read Dr. Clayton's evaluations of over 150 titles.

Cobb, C.G. *The Bad Times Primer.* Los Angeles: Times Publishing, $14.95. Available from Survival, Inc. Should be very useful but did not arrive in time to review.

The Great Survival Resource Book. Edited by M.A. Henderson and the editors of Paladin Press. Boulder, CO: Paladin Press, 1980. $14.95. Contains articles by some of the best known survival experts. Mel writes on "Survival Guns," Rick Fines on "Survival Vehicles," Bruce Clayton on "Nuclear Survival," etc. Good access to information sections. Since the book covers so many topics, it is not definitive, nor does it try to be, but it is a good introduction to the subject.

Kearny, Cresson. *Nuclear War Survival Skills.* Phoenix: Research Publications, P.O. Box 39850, Phoenix, AZ 85069. $19.95. Written by a former head researcher on civil defense at the Oak Ridge National Laboratory, this book contains do-it-yourself projects that the author and fellow researchers found practical during extensive field tests.

Retreat Location
Espenshade, Edward B., Jr., and Joel Morrison (eds.). *Goode's World Atlas,* 15th Edition. Chicago: Rand McNally, 1978. $10.95. This atlas is an indispensable aid to anyone seriously thinking about relocating to a safer area. Contains easy-to-read thematic maps giving population densities, agricultural, climatic and economic information.

The Whole Earth Atlas. Hammond, Inc., 1978. $6.95. Similar to *Goode's World Atlas* but not nearly as comprehensive.

TR-82 High Risk Areas For Civil Preparedness Nuclear Defense Planning Purposes. Prepared by Defense Civil Preparedness Agency. The Pentagon, Washington, D.C. 20301. Detailed maps of each state showing those areas considered high risk areas from direct weapons effects and/or high-level radioactive fallout.

Analyses of Effects of Limited Nuclear Warfare. Printed for the use of the Committee on Foreign Relations. U.S. Government Printing Office, Washington, D.C., 1975. 57-8520. Excellent maps showing the effects of nuclear attack on each state.

After you decide where you want to relocate, contact the state university press of your chosen home and ask them to send you their atlas of the state. In one volume you will have virtually all the facts you need to know about your area.

Other

Tappan, Mel. *Survival Guns.* Rogue River, OR: The Janus Press, 1980. $9.95. Read Mel's comments on page 183.

The Next Whole Earth Catalog. Edited by Stewart Brand. New York: Random House, 1980. $12.50. Indispensable source of information for anyone trying to develop a more self-sufficient life style.

Newsletters

There are several newsletters that should be important to the survivalist. Most of the so-called "hard money" newsletters deal with financial matters but those listed below contain information of particular interest to the survivalist. I urge you to subscribe to the *Duck Book* so that you can sample the entire range of newsletters available and decide which ones best suit your circumstances. Newsletter subscription prices may seem high but their publishers accept no advertising and their circulation is, for the most part, small.

Daily News Digest. Research Publications, P.O. Box 39850, Phoenix, AZ 85069. $150 per year, 5-week trial—$19. A weekly publication that contains excerpts from a wide variety of news sources not readily available to the average citizen.

The Reaper. R.E. McMaster, Jr., ed., P.O. Box 39026, Phoenix, AZ 85069. $225 per year, 5-issue trial—$25. Although *The Reaper* is written for those who are interested in commodities, the editor's "Cosmos" section is often thought provoking and resident weather expert Cliff Harris is regarded by many as the best in the business.

Gary North's Remnant Review. P.O. Box 39800, Phoenix, AZ 85069. $95 per year. Although he sometimes disagreed with Dr. North on personal survival matters, Mel regarded his economic views highly and thought his newsletter one of the most useful for the citizen of ordinary means seeking practical economic advice.

The Duck Book. Robert White, ed. Robert White, Inc., P.O. Box 1928, Cocoa Beach, FL 32922. Lifetime subscription (R. White's life, not yours)—$10. Gary North calls this publication "an information hand grenade." Each issue contains several excerpts from or entire issues of the various "hard money" newsletters. A bargain.

Personal Survival Letter. P.O. Box 598, Rogue River, OR 97537. $125 per year. Before he died, Mel founded and edited *P.S. Letter* which specializes in detailed, in-depth articles on different aspects of long-term survival— from medicine to weapons to mini-farming. Designed as a reference tool.

Survival Tomorrow. 901 N. Washington St., Suite 605, Alexandria, VA 22314. $30 for 12 issues. Karl Hess, who edits and writes for *Survival Tomorrow*, is well worth reading and he sees that each issue contains useful information.

Magazines

I have included only five publications here because you either may not know of them or hadn't thought of them in the survival context, but there are many others, especially regional and topical magazines, that will be of help to you as you begin to implement your preparations.

Co-Evolution Quarterly. P.O. Box 428, Sausalito, CA 94966. $14 per year. A mini-*Whole Earth Catalog* that comes out four times a year. Stimulating, some say "far-out," articles.

Mother Earth News. P.O. Box 70, Hendersonville, NC 28791. $15 per year. Although many of its articles offer unrealistic answers to problems, there is still a wealth of information on self-sufficient living to be found in *Mother's* pages.

Shotgun News. P.O. Box 669, Hastings, NE 68901. $9.50 per year. The place to find bargains on survival gear.

Survive. P.O. Box 49, Englewood, CO 80151. 12 issues for $22. A good introduction to the concept of survival—long as well as short-term.

The Survivor. Atlan Formularies, P.O. Box 327, Harrison, AR 72601. Bound Volumes I-IV, $40.00. Volume V soon to be released. Kurt Saxon, the editor, believes that when the system collapses, we can use late 19th century technology and survive in style. Useful information.